★ ICONS

70ˢ CARS

Vintage Auto Ads

Ed. Jim Heimann

Introduction by Tony Thacker

TASCHEN

KÖLN LONDON LOS ANGELES MADRID PARIS TOKYO

Front cover: Dodge Charger, 1970
Back cover: Volvo 164, 1974
Endpapers: Chevelle Malibu, 1970
Facing title page: Chevrolet Trucks, 1970

All images are from the Jim Heimann collection unless otherwise noted.
Any omissions for copyright or credit are unintentional and appropriate credit
will be given in future editions if such copyright holders contact the publisher.

**Dates in captions refer to the year of the advertisement's publication and not
necessarily the year in which the car/product was manufactured.**

To stay informed about upcoming TASCHEN titles, please request our magazine at
www.taschen.com/magazine or write to TASCHEN, Hohenzollernring 53, D-50672
Cologne, Germany, contact@taschen.com, Fax: +49-221-254919. We will be happy to
send you a free copy of our magazine, which is filled with information about all of
our books.

© 2006 TASCHEN GmbH
Hohenzollernring 53, D-50672 Köln
www.taschen.com

Editor: Jim Heimann, Los Angeles
Cover & interior design: Stephen Schmidt / Duuplex, San Mateo
Production: Morgan Slade, Los Angeles
Project management: Florian Kobler & Barbara Huttrop, Cologne
English-language editors: Kate Soto & Valerie Palmer, Los Angeles
German translation: Anke Burger, Berlin
French translation: Annie Berthold, Strasbourg

Printed in Italy
ISBN 3-8228-4800-X

Don't Be Fuelish

By Tony Thacker

The 1970s marked a unique period of transition between the psychedelic sixties and the consumption-crazed eighties. The so-called Me Decade ushered in a new penny-wise yet style-conscious consumer, more concerned with gas mileage than muscle in their cars. As the gas-guzzlers of the sixties gave way to the Gremlins of the seventies, the American auto industry found itself out of step with the buying public. Hustling to gauge changing public interests, Detroit created car fads as short-lived as pet rocks and lava lamps, and as quirky as the decade itself.

At the dawn of the seventies, the U.S. auto industry was booming at the rate of 6.5 million units per year. Ford president Lee Iacocca aggressively pursued the market, combining muscle-car power with sports-car handling. As a result, Ford sales topped the 3 million mark for the first time. The high-power trend was exemplified by Cadillac, which boasted the world's largest-capacity engine: 500 cubic inches (8,194 cubic cm), more than four times larger than the average Honda. Chrysler's Hemi 426 was the world's most powerful automobile engine with 425 horsepower. The muscle car was at its peak. The Plymouth Hemi Superbird was a full-blown, street-legal NASCAR race car for just $3,600.

While Detroit continued to flex its muscles with huge, gas-guzzling ships of the highway, foreign automakers began to discover significant markets in the United States for their well-engineered, thrifty cars. Volkswagen's U.S. sales peaked in 1970 with 569,000 units. Toyota and Nissan eventually began passing Volkswagen, and soon, one out of every four units sold in America was Japanese. To compete, the Big Three—Chrysler, Ford, and General Motors—all scrambled to add a few compacts to their rosters, such as Ford's Maverick. Known collectively as "pony" cars, most turned out to be donkeys.

Despite these early attempts to counter the flood of imports, Detroit did not sufficiently foresee the extent of the threat and continued with its production of large powerhouses. Ford upgraded the 1950s design of its Ranchero, and reintroduced the car as the first luxury pickup. It was really a car with a pickup bed replacing the back seat and trunk. Unfortunately, it was still a gas guzzler—efficiency was not yet in Ford's vocabulary.

When the flow of Middle East oil began to dry up with the 1973 OPEC-led embargo, driving culture began to change. Oil rationing and high fuel costs began to affect Americans, and as lines at gas pumps grew long, tempers ran short. Speed limits were lowered to 55 mph to save fuel. The Ad Council, the leading producer of U.S. public service announcements, developed a new energy-conservation campaign motto: "Don't Be Fuelish."

During this time, the euphoria of the muscle-car boom was beginning to fade under pressure from public safety groups and insurance companies who issued higher premiums for these cars because of their inefficient handling. And with stricter air-pollution laws, environmental groups pushed for more efficient engines. The 4-4-2 engine (four-on-the-floor transmission, four-barrel carb, and twin exhausts) that had given sixties' cars their power was no longer factory-standard. The Mustang and other ex-muscle machines were turning to flab.

Seizing the opportunity, Japanese and European automakers began carving unique niches for themselves in the U.S. market. Importers such as Datsun advertised their frugal "50 mpg highway/37 mpg city"—figures American manufacturers are still struggling to match. Honda, sensing a cultural shift and reaching out for a new

Top: *Ford Mustang Hardtop, 1971*   Bottom: *Porsche Targa, 1973*

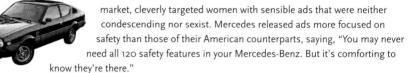

market, cleverly targeted women with sensible ads that were neither condescending nor sexist. Mercedes released ads more focused on safety than those of their American counterparts, saying, "You may never need all 120 safety features in your Mercedes-Benz. But it's comforting to know they're there."

In typical fashion, Cadillac had its own answer to the fuel crisis. In 1975 they unveiled the international-sized Seville, dubbed the "baby" Caddy. Unable to compete, Chrysler laid its Imperial to rest, and sales at the company continued to decline. Even Chevrolet dropped the 454-cubic-inch (7,440 cubic cm) motor from its Corvette Stingray. Catalytic converters were fitted to most cars and unleaded gasoline was mandated. Five mile-per-hour plastic bumpers now hung in place of the chrome chariot bumpers of the sixties.

One company trying to get it right was American Motors, leading the pack of subcompacts with the Gremlin in 1970 and the Pacer in 1975. Essentially a fish bowl, the Pacer was billed as the first wide, small car. At 77 inches (196 cm) across, it had girth. It also had acres of glass, a European-style hatchback, and an oversized passenger door. Its eccentric style and lack of power made it a short-lived phenomenon, but it remains nevertheless an icon of the decade.

Big cars, however, were Detroit's specialty, and the Big Three threw their efforts into the van craze, which swept American teens in the mid-seventies. Often customized with shag carpets and bead curtains, vans were traveling clubhouses for groovy teenagers across the country. Volkswagen followed the trend with its minibus and advertised, "It's more fun to take the bus." Likewise, sales of recreational vehicles such as the futuristic GMC increased.

Detroit was much less successful, however, at satisfying public demand for efficient reliable compacts. Unable to compete in the small-car segment, Ford laid its Maverick to rest. The auto giant's Pinto didn't fare much better. Built from 1971 to 1976, the popular compact became notorious for its rear-mounted fuel tank, which resulted in numerous fires and explosions from rear-end collisions. English automakers struggled too. Despite having a loyal following, Jaguars were idiosyncratic at best and unreliable at worst. Their electrical systems were built by a company called Joseph Lucas, later dubbed "Lucas: Prince of Darkness" by auto enthusiasts because the lights rarely worked.

Hollywood, on the other hand, was excellent at gauging consumer desires, and delivered car-centric entertainment that turned some seventies' cars into world-class icons. Volkswagen sales were boosted by a 1977 sequel to the sixties' hit film about a spunky Beetle, *Herbie Goes to Monte Carlo*. Ford's popular Torino could be seen in action from 1975 to 1979 on TV's weekly *Starsky and Hutch*. In 1976, Ford cashed in on its popularity and created a limited-edition Torino, which sported the famous cop car's shiny-red paint job and white stripe. Pontiac's Firebird Trans Am achieved fame in the Burt Reynolds 1977 movie *Smokey and the Bandit*. The action-packed film featured a black Trans Am with a giant golden eagle on the hood and helped double Trans Am sales from 46,000 in 1976 to 93,000 in 1978.

Despite the decade's fuel concerns, power was still in demand, and in 1979 millions of gearheads went to see *Mad Max*, which featured a young Mel Gibson as a brooding highway patrolman in a supercharged Ford Falcon GT XB, appropriately set during a time when gas had run out. Also that year, Bo and Luke began jumping their iconic Dodge Charger "General Lee"

Top: *Plymouth Arrow, 1977*   Middle: *Pontiac Firebird, 1977*   Bottom: *Ford Ranchero/77, 1977*

across TV screens weekly in *The Dukes of Hazzard*. Over the course of the show's six-year run, more than two hundred 1968–69 Chargers were destroyed.

While Hollywood made celebrities out of cars, some of Detroit's car execs were becoming famous on their own. In a surprise move that shocked the auto world, Ford stalwart Lee Iacocca resigned in 1978 and moved across town to a company with terminal cancer—Chrysler. Through sheer tenacity, top dog Iacocca would bring the company back from the auto-wrecking yard. At GM, John De Lorean's resignation earlier in the decade also made waves. The outspoken vice-president was openly critical of Detroit, accusing car companies of deliberately selling substandard transportation designs to consumers. De Lorean went on to found his own eponymous company, eventually producing the futuristic gull-winged De Lorean in 1981, which marked the transition toward a new generation of sleeker cars.

Throughout the seventies, carmakers struggled with the changing environment both in terms of legislation and the public's taste. By the decade's end, Detroit was beginning to shift gears, and style and aerodynamics were the new buzzwords. Computerized engine-management systems helped the industry meet public demand for both power and efficiency. In 1979, Ford developed a sporty concept car called the Probe 1, replacing the bulky rear-wheel drive typical of seventies' cars with a more-manageable front-wheel drive. A departure from the automaker's tissue-box angular production cars, Probe 1's stylish fuel-efficiency paved the way for cars to come.

Top: *Toyota Corolla, 1976*   Bottom: *Lincoln Versailles, 1978*

Ständig an die Tanke?
Nein danke!

Einleitung von Tony Thacker

Die 1970er-Jahre waren einzigartig, aber im Grunde eine Übergangszeit zwischen den psychedelischen 1960ern und dem Konsumrausch der 1980er. Sie wurden in den USA » das Ich-Jahrzehnt « genannt; die Verbraucher waren zugleich sparsam und modebewusst und hatten mehr Interesse am günstigen Benzinverbrauch als an Pferdestärken. Die Spritfresser der 1960er-Jahre wichen den Gremlins der 1970er, doch die amerikanische Autoindustrie merkte zu spät, dass sie den Draht zu den Käufern verloren hatte. Detroit bemühte sich daraufhin hektisch, dem veränderten Publikumsgeschmack hinterherzukommen und kreierte Automodelle, die ähnlich kurzlebig und schrullig waren wie Lavalampen und die Les Humphries Singers.

Zu Beginn der 1970er-Jahre boomte die US-Autoindustrie noch mit einem Ausstoß von 6,5 Mio. Fahrzeugen pro Jahr. Der Ford-Präsident Lee Iacocca hatte das Ohr am Puls der Zeit und kombinierte die Leistung der Muscle Cars mit dem Fahrgefühl eines Sportwagens. Das führte dazu, dass Ford zum ersten Mal die 3-Millionen-Marke überschreiten konnte. Cadillac bot das beste Beispiel für den Trend zu hohen PS-Zahlen und konnte sich mit dem größten Hubraum der Welt brüsten: 8.194 Kubikzentimeter, mehr als viermal größer als beim durchschnittlichen Honda. Der Chrysler Hemi 426 hatte mit 425 PS den stärksten Automotor der Welt unter der Haube. Die Muscle Cars waren so populär wie nie. Mit dem Plymouth Hemi Superbird konnte man einen waschechten, für die Straße zugelassenen NASCAR-Rennwagen für läppische 3.600 Dollar erstehen.

Während Detroit weiter mit riesigen, spritsaufenden Straßenkreuzern die Muskeln spielen ließ, boten sich für ausländische Autohersteller und ihre gut konstruierten, sparsamen Wagen wichtige Nischen. Volkswagen erreichte 1970 mit 569.000 Stück seine besten Verkaufszahlen in den USA. Toyota und Nissan liefen Volkswagen jedoch schnell den Rang ab, bald stammte jedes vierte in Amerika verkaufte Auto aus Japan. The Big Three – Chrysler, Ford und General Motors – versuchten mitzuhalten und ebenfalls ein paar Kleinwagen wie den Ford Maverick auf den Markt zu werfen. Diese als » Pony Cars « bezeichneten Wagen erwiesen sich zum größten Teil jedoch nicht als » Mustangs «, sondern als lahme Esel.

Trotz dieser frühen Versuche, sich der Importflut entgegenzustemmen, konnte Detroit das wahre Ausmaß der Bedrohung nicht erkennen und machte einfach mit der Produktion der dicken Muskelpakete weiter. Ford verbesserte das 1950er-Jahre-Design seines Ranchero und brachte den Wagen als ersten Luxus-Pickup auf den Markt. Er war im Grunde ein Pkw, bei dem Rücksitz und Kofferraum durch eine Kleintransporter-Ladefläche ersetzt wurden. Leider hatte er nach wie vor mächtigen Benzindurst – das Wort Rentabilität gab es im Ford-Vokabular noch nicht.

Als der Nachschub an Öl aus dem Nahen Osten 1973 mit dem Ölembargo der OPEC austrocknete, begann sich das amerikanische Fahrverhalten zu ändern. Ölrationierungen und hohe Benzinpreise trafen alle Amerikaner, die Schlangen an den Zapfsäulen wurden immer länger, die Nerven immer angespannter. Um Benzin zu sparen, wurde das Tempolimit auf 90 km/h verringert. Das Ad Council, wichtigster Produzent öffentlicher Durchsagen im amerikanischen Radio, entwickelte eine Energiespar-Kampagne unter dem Motto » Don't Be Fuelish « (Sei nicht dumm, spar Benzin.)

Top: *Honda Civic, 1974*   Bottom: *Ford Torino, 1972*

Aus dem Muscle-Car-Hype war endgültig die Luft heraus, als Verbraucherschützer Druck machten und Versicherungsgesellschaften wegen des ineffizienten Fahrverhaltens höhere Prämien für diese Wagen verlangten. Mit der Einführung strengerer Luftreinhaltungsgesetze drängten Umweltschutzgruppen auf Motoren mit niedrigerem Verbrauch. Der »4-4-2-Motor« (4-Gang-Knüppelschaltung, Vierzylinder-Vergaser und Doppelauspuff), der den 1960er-Jahre-Schlitten so viel Power gegeben hatte, war keine Standardausstattung mehr. Der Mustang und andere ehemalige Muskelpakete setzten Fett an.

Die japanischen und europäischen Autohersteller ließen sich nicht lange bitten und begannen wichtige Nischen auf dem amerikanischen Markt für sich zu erobern. Importwagen wie der Datsun warben mit ihrem sparsamen Verbrauch von 5 Litern auf der Autobahn und 6,7 Litern in der Stadt – Zahlen, denen die amerikanischen Hersteller heute noch nichts entgegensetzen können. Honda hatte ein gutes Gespür für die kulturellen Veränderungen und sprach Frauen mit cleveren Anzeigen an, die weder herablassend noch sexistisch waren. Mercedes legte in seiner Werbung mehr Wert auf Sicherheit als die Amerikaner: »Wahrscheinlich werden Sie nie alle 120 Sicherheitsmerkmale Ihres Mercedes-Benz brauchen. Aber es ist beruhigend zu wissen, dass es sie gibt.«

Cadillac fand seine ganz eigene, typische Antwort auf die Kraftstoffkrise: 1975 wurde der auf internationale Maße geschrumpfte Seville, genannt der »Baby Caddy«, präsentiert. Chrysler konnte da nicht mithalten und schickte den Imperial in die ewigen Jagdgründe, die Verkaufszahlen des Unternehmens gingen immer weiter in den Keller. Sogar Chevrolet baute die Corvette Stingray nun ohne den 7,4-Liter-Motor. Die meisten Autos wurden jetzt mit Katalysatoren ausgestattet, an den Zapfsäulen gab es nur noch bleifreies Benzin. Schlabberige Plastikstoßstangen wurden an die Stelle der verchromten Kuhfänger aus den 1960er-Jahren gehängt.

Ein Unternehmen, das es richtig zu machen versuchte, war American Motors, die das Rudel der Kleinwagen 1970 mit dem Gremlin und 1975 mit dem Pacer anführten. Der Pacer sah aus wie ein Goldfischglas und wurde als »the first wide small car« (der erste geräumige Kleinwagen) angepriesen. Mit seinen 196 cm Breite hatte er einen beträchtlichen Leibesumfang, Unmengen von Fensterflächen, ein europäisches Fließheck und eine extragroße Beifahrertür. Sein exzentrisches Styling und die geringe Leistung ließen ihn zu einem kurzlebigen Phänomen werden, aber er blieb dennoch eine der Ikonen dieses Jahrzehnts.

Detroits Spezialität blieben jedoch große Autos; die Big Three richteten ihre gesamte Energie auf die Kleinbusse, die Mitte der 1970er-Jahre bei Jugendlichen der letzte Schrei waren. Die Busse wurden oft mit Flokatiteppich und Perlenvorhang ausgestattet und waren im ganzen Land als fahrende Discos für groovende Teenager unterwegs. Volkswagen stieg mit seinem Bus in den Trend ein und warb mit dem Slogan: »Bus fahren macht mehr Spaß.« Auch die Verkaufszahlen von Freizeitmobilen wie dem futuristischen GMC nahmen zu.

Detroit schaffte es jedoch nicht, die Nachfrage nach effizienten, zuverlässigen Kompaktwagen zu befriedigen. Ford konnte im Kleinwagen-Segment nicht länger mithalten und stellte die Produktion des Maverick ein. Dem Pinto des Autogiganten erging es nicht wesentlich besser. Er wurde von 1971 bis 1976 gebaut, erwarb sich jedoch einen zweifelhaften Ruf wegen seines im Heck angebrachten Tanks, der bei Auffahrunfällen zu

zahlreichen Feuerausbrüchen und Explosionen führte. Auch die englischen Autobauer hatten zu knabbern. Trotz seiner treuen Anhängerschaft war der Jaguar bestenfalls eigenwillig und schlimmstenfalls unzuverlässig. Seine Elektronik wurde von der Firma Joseph Lucas gebaut, die sich unter Kfz-Fans den Beinamen »Lucas: Fürst der Finsternis« erwarb, weil die Lichter meistens nicht funktionierten.

Hollywood hatte keinerlei Probleme damit, die Verbraucherwünsche zu erkennen, und produzierte Filme rund ums Auto, mit denen etliche 1970er-Jahre-Wagen zu weltweit bekannten Kultobjekten wurden. Die VW-Verkäufe wurden von der 1977er-Fortsetzung des 1960er-Jahre-Hitfilms über den frechen Käfer Herbie *Ein toller Käfer in der Rallye Monte Carlo* ordentlich angekurbelt. Der beliebte Ford Torino war von 1975 bis 1979 in *Starsky and Hutch* allwöchentlich in Aktion zu sehen. 1976 nutzte Ford seine Popularität aus und brachte ein Torino-Sondermodell mit derselben knallroten Lackierung und weißem Rallyestreifen wie beim Wagen der berühmten Cops heraus. Auch der Pontiac Firebird Trans-Am wurde 1977 mit dem Burt-Reynolds-Film *Ein ausgekochtes Schlitzohr* unsterblich. In dem Actionfilm kam ein schwarzer Trans-Am mit einem riesigen goldenen Adler auf der Haube vor und führte zur Verdopplung der Trans-Am-Verkaufszahlen von 46.000 im Jahr 1976 auf 93.000 im Jahr 1978.

Trotz der Benzinprobleme des Jahrzehnts waren leistungsstarke Wagen immer noch gefragt und Millionen von Technikfetischisten sahen sich 1979 *Mad Max* an, in dem ein junger Mel Gibson einen übellaunigen Polizisten in einem superausgestatteten Ford Falcon GT XB spielt, in einer Zukunft, in der es kein Benzin mehr gibt. Im selben Jahr begannen Bo und Luke mit ihrem kultigen Dodge Charger »General Lee« jede Woche in *Ein Duke kommt selten allein* über die Mattscheibe zu krachen. Im Laufe der sechs Jahre, in denen die Serie lief, wurden über zweihundert 1968–69er Charger geschrottet.

Während in Hollywood die Autos die Stars waren, gelangten in Detroit einige der Autoindustrie-Kapitäne ebenfalls zu Ruhm. In einem Überraschungsschachzug, der der Autowelt einen Schock versetzte, trat der altgediente Ford-Chef Lee Iacocca 1978 von seinem Posten zurück und fing schräg gegenüber bei einem eigentlich schon totgesagten Unternehmen an – bei Chrysler. Durch schiere Hartnäckigkeit schaffte es der geniale Iacocca, die Firma vor dem Schrottplatz der Geschichte zu retten. Bei GM hatte der Rücktritt von John De Lorean ebenfalls Wellen geschlagen. Der Ex-Vizepräsident des Unternehmens hatte die amerikanische Autoindustrie offen kritisiert und den Herstellern vorgeworfen, den Verbrauchern willentlich minderwertiges Kfz-Design zu verkaufen. Daraufhin gründete De Lorean eine Firma unter eigenem Namen, die 1981 den futuristischen DeLorean Flügeltürer herausbrachte, ein Meilenstein in der Entwicklung hin zu einer neuen Generation eleganterer Autos.

Das gesamte Jahrzehnt hindurch kämpften die Kfz-Hersteller mit einem Umfeld, in dem sich sowohl die Gesetzgebung als auch der Geschmack der autofahrenden Öffentlichkeit ständig veränderte. Erst Ende der 1970er legte Detroit einen anderen Gang ein, Gestaltung und Aerodynamik waren die neuen Schlagworte. Computergesteuerte Maschinenanlagen halfen der Industrie dabei, die Nachfrage nach Kraft und Effizienz zugleich zu befriedigen. 1979 entwickelte Ford ein sportliches Konzeptauto mit dem Namen Concept Probe 1, bei dem der für die 1970er-Jahre-Autos typische, sperrige Hinterradantrieb durch einen handlicheren Vorderradantrieb ersetzt wurde. Concept Probe 1 läutete den Abschied von der eckigen Schuhkartonform für Ford ein und bahnte mit seinem modischen Stil und sparsamen Verbrauch den Weg für die Autos der Zukunft.

Top: *Oldsmobile Delta 88, 1970*   Bottom: *Mercury, 1970*

Carburez malin !

Introduction par Tony Thacker

Les années 1970 ont été une décennie unique, le passage des Sixties psychédéliques aux années 1980 consuméristes. La décennie du « Et moi ? Et moi ? Et moi ? » a ouvert la voie à un nouveau consommateur, économe mais pas moins esthète, qui, quand il s'agit de voiture, s'inquiète davantage de la consommation de son moteur que de sa puissance. Lorsque les voraces des années 1960 ont laissé la place aux diablotins des Seventies, l'industrie automobile américaine s'est trouvée en décalage avec sa clientèle. Detroit s'est démenée pour jauger les humeurs changeantes du public et a lancé des engouements automobiles aussi éphémères et flamboyants que la mode du « caillou domestique » (le fameux *pet-rock*) ou celle de la lampe à lave, des modèles aussi extravagants que l'époque elle-même.

À l'aube des années 1970, l'industrie automobile américaine est en plein boum : 6,5 millions de voitures sortent chaque année de ses usines. Le président de Ford, Lee Iacocca, se lance à l'assaut du marché : en combinant la puissance des moteurs gonflés à la maniabilité des voitures de sport, il fait franchir à Ford, pour la première fois, le seuil des trois millions d'unités vendues. La mode des voitures puissantes est incarnée par Cadillac qui a lancé, à sa grande fierté, la plus grosse cylindrée du monde avec 8 194 centimètres cubes, soit des cylindres quatre fois plus grands que ceux d'une Honda de base. La Hemi 426 de Chrysler porte alors sous son capot le moteur le plus puissant, un 425 chevaux. Les engins gonflés sont à leur apogée. Avec la Plymouth Hemi Superbird, le consommateur américain peut s'offrir une stock-car routière gonflée à bloc pour 3 600 dollars.

Tandis que Detroit continue à submerger le marché avec ses bulldozers de l'asphalte, les constructeurs étrangers découvrent un marché américain qui se révèle friand de ses petites voitures bien assemblées et économiques. Les ventes de Volkswagen États-Unis culminent en 1970 avec 569 000 unités. Toyota et Nissan parviennent ensuite à dépasser Volkswagen et, très vite, une voiture sur quatre vendue en Amérique est japonaise. Pour résister à cette concurrence, les « Trois Grands » – Chrysler, Ford, et General Motors – se hâtent d'ajouter quelques compactes à leur catalogue, comme la Maverick de Ford. Celles qu'on a baptisé les « pony cars » se sont souvent révélées des mulets.

Malgré ces premières tentatives pour contrer le déluge des voitures importées, Detroit ne prévoit pas l'étendue de la menace et continue à produire des locomotives pour autoroute. Ford modernise le design très années 1950 de sa Ranchero et la relance comme première camionnette de luxe. C'est en fait une voiture dotée d'un plateau à la place de la plage arrière et du coffre, et, hélas, encore un gouffre à carburant : le mot « rendement » ne fait pas encore partie du vocabulaire de Ford.

Lorsque les flots de pétrole du Proche-Orient viennent à se tarir avec l'embargo imposé par l'OPEP en 1973, la culture automobile commence à changer. Les rationnements d'essence et les prix élevés du pétrole atteignent les Américains et leur patience s'amenuise à mesure que s'allongent les files d'attente dans les stations-service.

La vitesse est limitée à 90 km/h pour économiser le carburant. L'Ad Council, premier producteur d'annonces publicitaires pour les services publics américains, lance une nouvelle campagne sur les économies d'énergie autour du slogan « Don't Be Fuelish »[1].

L'euphorie qui avait accompagné l'explosion des muscle cars commence alors à s'estomper sous la pression de groupements d'intérêt public et des compagnies d'assurance qui leur imposent des primes

Top: *Mercury Cougar, 1971*   Bottom: *Ford Mustang Mach 1, 1972*

supérieures en raison de leur maniement difficile. Les lois anti-pollution se multiplient et les groupes écologistes militent pour des moteurs plus économiques. Le moteur 4-4-2 (quatre vitesses au plancher, carburateur quadruple corps et double ligne d'échappement) qui avait donné leur puissance aux voitures des années 1960 n'est plus compatible avec les chaînes d'usines. La Mustang et ses consœurs musclées commencent à se ramollir.

Se précipitant sur l'occasion, les constructeurs japonais et européens se constituent peu à peu des niches sur le marché américain. Des importées comme les Datsun se vendent sur le slogan minimaliste « 5 litres aux cent sur autoroute / 10 litres aux cent en ville » – des chiffres que les constructeurs américains tentent toujours d'atteindre. Honda, qui sent venir un glissement culturel et recherche un nouveau marché, cible très habilement les femmes avec des spots qui évitent judicieusement condescendance et sexisme. Mercedes propose des campagnes plus centrées sur la sécurité, en lançant au consommateur : « Vous n'aurez peut-être jamais besoin des 120 dispositifs de sécurité de votre Mercedes-Benz. Mais c'est rassurant de savoir qu'ils existent. »

Cadillac, fidèle à sa réputation, fournit sa propre réponse à la crise pétrolière. En 1975, sa direction dévoile la Seville internationale, surnommée la « Baby Caddy ». Dépassé, Chrysler range son Imperial au placard et ses ventes continuent leur déclin. Même Chevrolet abandonne le moteur 454 de sa Corvette Stingray. Les convertisseurs catalytiques sont mis en place sur la plupart des voitures et l'essence sans plomb est autorisée à la vente. Des pare-chocs en plastique remplacent les chromes des Sixties.

Il y a bien une marque américaine qui a essayé de faire les choses correctement : American Motors lance la vogue des sub-compactes avec la Gremlin en 1970 et la Pacer en 1975. Sorte d'aquarium sur roues, l'AMC Pacer est décrite comme la première petite voiture spacieuse. Ses 196 cm de largeur lui donnent du ventre. Elle est aussi équipée d'un vaste dôme vitré à l'arrière, d'un petit capot plongeant, d'un hayon arrière (alors rarissime aux États-Unis) et d'une portière gauche plus longue de 10 cm. Son style excentrique ne suffisant pas à compenser sa motorisation désuète et son manque de brio, le phénomène est de courte durée, mais la silhouette de la Pacer reste l'une des icônes de cette époque[2].

Les grosses bagnoles restent malgré tout la spécialité de Detroit et les « Big Three » se jettent à corps perdu dans la folie de la camionnette qui transporte les ados américains au milieu des années 1970. Souvent personnalisées, décorées de tapis moelleux et de rideaux de perles, les camionnettes sont les nids d'amour ambulants des jeunes branchés de tout le pays. Volkswagen suit la tendance et lance son minibus avec le slogan « C'est plus marrant de prendre le bus ». Dans la même veine, on voit augmenter les ventes de véhicules récréatifs, comme la futuriste GMC.

Detroit ne parvient en revanche pas à satisfaire le goût du public pour les compactes économiques et rassurantes. Incapable de rester compétitif dans le secteur des petites voitures, Ford gare sa Maverick en maison de retraite. Sa Pinto ne durera pas plus longtemps. Construite entre 1971 et 1976, cette compacte populaire est connue à cause de son réservoir arrière qui a causé plusieurs incendies et explosions après des collisions.

Les constructeurs anglais luttent aussi pour rester dans la bataille. Les Jaguar ont des adeptes fidèles, mais il faut bien avouer qu'elles sont au mieux spéciales et au pire très peu fiables. Leur système électrique est assemblé par la société Joseph Lucas, plus tard rebaptisée « Lucas : Prince des Ténèbres » par les amateurs de belle carrosserie, parce que les phares ne fonctionnaient que rarement. Hollywood est un excellent instrument de mesure, et d'encouragement, des désirs du public : la voiture occupe un rôle central dans

Top: *Toyota Corolla, 1970*   Bottom: *Ford Thunderbird, 1970*

l'industrie du divertissement, qui a fait de certains modèles des années 1970 des idoles planétaires. Les ventes de Volkswagen explosent par exemple en 1977 grâce à l'histoire au parfum très sixties d'*Un Amour de Coccinelle* (*Herbie Goes to Monte Carlo*). La

Torino de Ford fuse à travers tous les épisodes de la série *Starsky et Hutch* entre 1975 et 1979. En 1976, Ford rentabilise cette vitrine et lance une édition limitée de la Torino, rouge flamboyant traversé d'une flèche blanche comme celle des deux flics « qui gagnent toujours à la fin ». La Firebird Trans Am de Pontiac conquiert la gloire en accueillant Burt Reynolds dans le film *Cours après moi Shérif* (*Smokey and the Bandit*, 1977). Ce film d'action viril présente sous son meilleur jour une Trans Am noire avec un immense aigle doré sur le capot, qui fait grimper les ventes du modèle de 46 000 en 1976 à 93 000 en 1978.

Malgré la crise du pétrole qui a marqué cette décennie, les consommateurs sont toujours en quête de puissance : en 1979, des millions de spectateurs vont voir *Mad Max*, dans lequel le jeune Mel Gibson incarne un ténébreux policier de la route qui parcourt des paysages désertiques à bord d'une Ford Falcon GT XB surcomprimée, à une époque, peut-être pas si lointaine, où il n'y a plus de pétrole. C'est aussi cette année-là que Bo et Luke grimpent pour la première fois dans leur Dodge Charger baptisée « General Lee » pour *Shérif, fais moi peur* ! Au cours des six années qu'a duré la série, plus de 200 Chargers de 1968 – 69 Chargers ont été détruites.

Hollywood transforme les voitures en stars, et certains patrons de l'industrie automobile accèdent aussi à la célébrité. Detroit tremble sur ses fondations en 1979 lorsque Lee Iacocca, fidèle parmi les fidèles, quitte brusquement Ford pour son concurrent à l'agonie – Chrysler. À force de ténacité, le maître Iacocca sauvera le constructeur de la casse. Chez General Motors, la démission de John De Lorean, quelques années plus tôt, a aussi fait des vagues. Le vice-président de GM n'avait pas sa langue dans sa poche et ne se gênait pas pour critiquer Detroit et accuser les constructeurs automobiles de vendre délibérément aux consommateurs des voitures de qualité insuffisante. De Lorean fonde son entreprise éponyme, qui mettra sur le marché en 1981 la futuriste De Lorean aux ailes en M, qui a marqué la transition vers une nouvelle génération de voitures plus élégantes.

Pendant les années 1970, les constructeurs automobiles se sont débattus dans un environnement en perpétuel changement, tant du point de vue des lois que des goûts du public. À la fin de la décennie, Detroit commence tout juste à reprendre de la vitesse en s'appuyant sur deux nouveaux maîtres mots : style et aérodynamisme. Les systèmes informatisés de contrôle du moteur aident l'industrie à s'aligner sur la demande du public en créant des voitures à la fois puissantes et économiques. En 1979, Ford développe une concept car sportive appelée Probe 1, avec laquelle il remplace la traction arrière corpulente, typique des années 1970, par une traction avant plus maniable. En rupture avec les voitures en boîte à chaussure qui ont fait la renommée de la marque, la Probe 1, racée et économique, aura nombre de descendantes dans les années 1980.

[1] Ce slogan, que l'on pourrait traduire par « carburez malin ! », joue de la consonance entre les mots *fuel* (essence) et *foolish* (idiot, ridicule, naïf...).

[2] Alors que sa mode s'épuise en Amérique, la Pacer jouit d'une deuxième carrière en France : des stars comme Brigitte Bardot et Coluche vantent les courbes de la petite américaine, qui devient brièvement la coqueluche du Tout Paris et se vend à 3 000 exemplaires dans l'Hexagone.

Top: *Ford Country Squire, 1970*   Middle: *Datsun B-210 GX, 1978*   Bottom: *Ford Thunderbird, 1977*

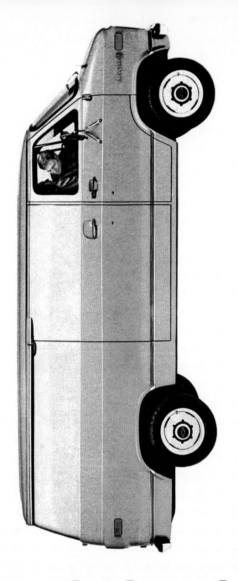

Chevrolet launches the space vehicle.
'71 Chevy Van.

FOR 1970:
A NEW FLIGHT
OF BIRDS

Soaring into the '70's far ahead of the rest...
1970 Thunderbird. With dramatic new front-
end styling, shaped to slice the wind.
Longer, lower and wider for '70. Yet, still uniquely
Thunderbird. With its impressive list of standard
luxury features you'd pay extra for in other
cars. Options other cars don't even offer. And
standards of quality most others only aspire to.
Choose from three distinctive models.
The New Flight of Birds is ready for take-off.

Above: Pan Am's Boeing 747 Jet and the 1970 Thunderbird
2-Door Landau with Special Brougham interior.

THUNDERBIRD *Ford*

Chevrolet Van, 1970 ◄

Ford Thunderbird, 1970

Better ideas make better cars: 1971 Mercury Montego.

One foot shorter than big cars for easier parking.

1. Start with the best ideas in intermediates.

The new Mercury Montego has them all. Handy parkable size: over a foot shorter than big cars. Popular price: the Mercury Montego MX 2-door hardtop shown is priced virtually the same as a similar size car built 10 years ago, before inflation.

2. Add extra room and luxury.

Mercury Montego is a full six-passenger car. Seats a family of six adults. The ride is smooth, comfortable, quiet. The trunk is vacation size (16.2 cu. ft.). Deluxe interiors are standard in cloth and vinyl, or all vinyl at no extra cost.

3. And you have a better luxury intermediate.

Mercury Montego comes in 12 models including two station wagons and three sporty Cyclones. The standard engine is a 250 CID "6" for Montegos with options to 351-4V V-8. The standard for Montego Cyclones is a 351 CID V-8 with options to 429-CJ 4V V-8. It takes better ideas to make better cars. Mercury makes better cars to buy, rent, or lease.

MERCURY

LINCOLN-MERCURY DIV. *Ford*

Pontiac, 1970 ◄

Mercury Montego, 1970   ►► Chevrolet Impala, 1972

We were talking about Charger, and your name came up.

Pontiac LeMans, 1971 ◄   *Dodge Charger, 1970* ►► *Dodge Charger, 1972*

1973 DO
Extra care in
a diffe

CHARGER COUPE WITH LANDAU TOP

CHARGER SE.

CHARGER HARDTOP WITH
HALO ROOF.

GE CHARGER.
ineering makes
ce in Dodge...depend on it.

Dodge

Dodge

Dodge Challenger...
The sports car that knows
how to treat a lady.

If you didn't know better, you'd almost think Challenger had been designed by a girl. Who else would have made it low and sporty-looking, but still big enough so you don't get that squashed feeling when you're inside? Aren't things like the sports-type steering wheel and sharp color-coordinated carpeting women's touches? Who but a member of the female sex would be smart enough to combine looks with practicality? Take those flush door handles. They aren't just for looks, you know. They're safer, too. And who but an economy-minded lady would have made those thrifty six- and eight-cylinder engines standard? Both use regular gas. Speaking of thrift, Challenger's price is pretty nice, too. If Challenger was designed by a man, I bet he talked to his girl first.

**If you think
all this was
worth waiting
for...
you could be
DODGE
MATERIAL.**

Dodge Challenger, 1970

Turn it on. Off the road.

The Harley-Davidson SX-350.
Leads an exciting double life.
Takes you, street-legal, to where the off-road action is.
Then busts loose with 350cc's metered through five selected ratios to move you 'cross the flat, up a hill, or through the rough.
With Ceriani front forks, 5-way adjustable rear shocks.
The frame: double down tube in keeping with its personality.
And sure electric start.
Quick off the line. On the road. Or off.

Harley-Davidson,
Milwaukee, Wisconsin 53201
Member Motorcycle Industry Council

AMF
Harley-Davidson

Harley-Davidson SX-350.
The Great American Freedom Machine.

Harley-Davidson SX-350, 1973 ▶▶ *Volkswagen, 1970*

We do our thing.

The funny thing is, we didn't even know we had a "thing".

We've been perfecting one car for 25 years, steering clear of the idiocy of annual model changes.

Our only worry has been how to make the VW work better, not look different.

And we haven't done badly at all: The 1970 VW is faster and quieter with a longer-lasting engine than any other beetle.

But you still need a scorecard to tell the '70 from other years. Or any year from any other year.

Nobody in the world makes and serv-ices a car as well as we do. Because no-body's been doing it as long on one model.

We still use old-fashioned words like "nifty," "peachy" and "swell".

And we stick to old-fashioned ideas like craftsmanship and dedication and skill.

You do yours.

Then, for $1839*, our thing becomes your
ng. And what happens is wild.
People treat VWs like something else.
They polish them, scrub them, stripe them
d flower them in very far-out ways.
Why? Why mostly on Volkswagens?
We think it's affection, pure and simple.

A VW is a new member of the family who
happens to live in the garage.
And when a VW moves in, people flip out.
Driving a VW, we are told, is a groove.
You don't get zapped with freaky running
costs. Or zonked with kinky maintenance
bills. Or clobbered with crazy depreciation.

We've built the VW durably enough to
withstand heat, cold, flood, snow, sand, mud.
Yet it's durable enough to withstand a
whole new generation.
Maybe you thought we were
in a rut. When all the time we were
really in the groove.

Born: The 12-cylinder animal

Jaguar, a breed of cat rarely considered timid, announces the most exciting automotive development in years—an aluminum V-12 engine.

The logic of the V-12 configuration: The V-12 is inherently balanced. Its smoothness is almost uncanny.

Significance: This 12-cylinder engine idles in near-silence. Its virtual absence of vibration may take some getting used to.

Some specifics: Jaguar's V-12 displaces only 326 cubic inches and yet develops 314 horsepower. The cylinders have a very large bore and the pistons have a short stroke, to attain higher potential power and longer engine life. And the power is delivered through an exceptionally wide range of engine revolutions.

An eye-opener: The ignition system is transistorized. It employs a new electronic distributor that eliminates all contact points. With no contact points to wear or foul, a major cause of engine tune-ups is eliminated. (Incidentally, an out of tune engine is a major cause of air pollution.)

Finally: Jaguar has a fully-independent suspension system with "anti-dive" front-end geometry. New disc brakes, power-assisted on all 4 wheels. And rack-and-pinion steering, also power assisted, with 3.5 turns lock-to-lock and a turning circle of 36 feet.

Incredibly, the Jaguar 2+2, with this revolutionary V-12 engine, costs only $7,325.*

See the 12-cylinder animal at your nearby Jaguar dealer. Study the engine. Because it's the one you'll be hearing about for many years to come.

For the name of your nearest Jaguar dealer, dial (800) 631-1971 except in New Jersey where the number is (800) 962-2803. Calls are toll-free.

British Leyland Motors Inc., Leonia, New Jersey 07605.

Jaguar V-12

*Manufacturer's suggested retail price, P.O.E. Destination charges, dealer preparation charges, state and local taxes (if any) not included. Whitewalls optional extra.

JAGUAR:
THE CAR THAT MAKES GREAT BRITAIN
A GREAT SPORTS CAR POWER
CAN MAKE YOU ONE TOO.

[FOR LESS THAN YOU THINK]

0-60 mph	6.7 sec.
0-100 mph	19.0 sec.
Standing 1/4 mile	15.3 sec.
Speed 1/4 mile	90 mph
Horsepower	245 bhp

Statistical Source: XK-E Roadster, Car and Driver, May, 1969

**FOR EXACT COMPARISONS [SPECIFICATIONS, PERFORMANCE, AND PRICE]
WITH OTHER GREAT SPORTS CAR POWERS, SEE YOUR JAGUAR DEALER.**

Studies show that excessive noise can bring on anxiety, bizarre bodily sensations and personality disintegration.

If you can afford a car you can afford two Gremlins.

Until April 1, 1970, only an imported economy car could make that statement.

Then American Motors introduced the Gremlin. And America had a car priced to compete with the imports. The two-passenger Gremlin lists for $1,879[1], the four-passenger for $1,959[1].

The Gremlin gets the best mileage of any car made in America. It goes about 500 miles on a tank of gas. It normally goes 6,000 miles between oil changes, 24,000 between lube jobs.

From bumper to bumper, it's just 2½ inches longer than a Volkswagen. Yet its turning circle is 3 feet less than VW's. Which makes the Gremlin about the easiest car in the world to park and handle.

For a car this size, the Gremlin does surprisingly well on expressways. It is 10 inches wider, 7 inches lower and 765 pounds heavier than a VW, which means a smoother more stable ride. And its 128 hp engine goes from 0 to 60 in 15.3 seconds.

Aside from all these practical advantages, the Gremlin gives you something no imported economy car could ever offer.

The fun of driving the new American car.

$1,959[1]
4-passenger

$1,879[1]
2-passenger

◢◤ American Motors

$3,986.65.*

CHRYSLER CHRYSLER
MOTORS CORPORATION

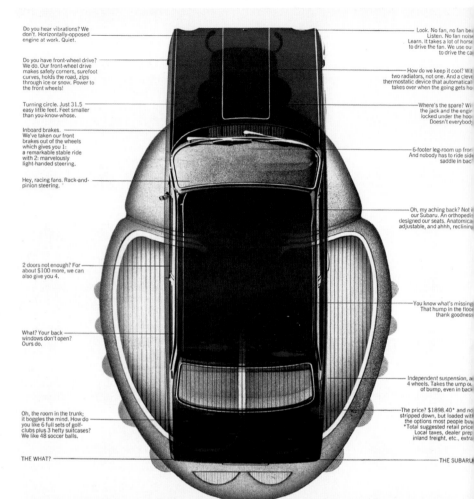

Do you hear vibrations? We don't. Horizontally-opposed engine at work. Quiet.

Do you have front-wheel drive? We do. Our front-wheel drive makes safety corners, surefoot curves, holds the road, zips through ice or snow. Power to the front wheels!

Turning circle. Just 31.5 easy little feet. Feet smaller than you-know-whose.

Inboard brakes. We've taken our front brakes out of the wheels which gives you 1: a remarkable stable ride with 2: marvelously light-handed steering.

Hey, racing fans. Rack-and-pinion steering.

2 doors not enough? For about $100 more, we can also give you 4.

What? Your back windows don't open? Ours do.

Oh, the room in the trunk; it boggles the mind. How do you like 6 full sets of golf-clubs plus 3 hefty suitcases? We like 48 soccer balls.

THE WHAT?

Look. No fan, no fan be Listen. No fan noise Learn. It takes a lot of horse to drive the fan. We use ou to drive the ca

How do we keep it cool? Wit two radiators, not one. And a cleve thermostatic device that automaticall takes over when the going gets ho

Where's the spare? Wi the jack and the engir locked under the hoo Doesn't everybody

6-footer leg-room up fron And nobody has to ride side saddle in bac

Oh, my aching back? Not i our Subaru. An orthopedis designed our seats. Anatomica adjustable, and ahhh, reclining

You know what's missing That hump in the floor thank goodness

Independent suspension, a 4 wheels. Takes the ump ou of bump, even in back

The price? $1898.40* and no stripped down, but loaded wit the options most people buy *Total suggested retail price Local taxes, dealer prep inland freight, etc., extra

THE SUBARU

The Subaru is not a Japanese Beetle

Subaru of America, Pennsauken, New Jersey 08109

At 70 mph it doesn't even breathe hard.

For dealer nearest you, call toll free: 800-631-4299. In New Jersey, 800-962-2803. Subaru. A product of Fuji Heavy Industries Ltd. Japan.

BEAT THE SYSTEM. BUY A VOLVO.

Out on the Mississippi, time drifts back 100 years. To the days when sternwheelers like the Delta Queen linked the river ports of mid-America.

Once aboard, you become part of the unchanging life on the river.

America. There's so much to see.

And you could hardly find a more dependable

way to see it than in the 1972 Chevy Nova.

Actually, this year's Nova is pretty much unchanged from last year's Nova. The car indepe auto mechanics said was "easiest to service" and had the "least mechanical problems." (Compared all cars, in a survey conducted by *Motor Service Service Station Management* magazines.)

1972 Nova Coupe with the famous Delta Queen riverboat on the Mississippi.

Chevrolet. Building a bette

Chevrolet Nova, 1972

keeps on rolling along.

With a car as dependable and economical as Nova, ~~you~~ don't go redoing it from one year to the next.

Mechanical improvements, yes. Like modifications ~~to~~ the generator, and in the rear axle, to make them ~~ev~~en more durable. And improved emission controls for ~~cl~~eaner air.

Let's just say we do what ought to be done.

Because we want your new Nova to be the best car you ever owned.

Take your family aboard the Nova for a trial run.

At your Chevy dealer's.

Chevrolet

way to see the U.S.A.

►► *Ford Country Squire, 1970*

Dear Dad:
This is why I want a
Suzuki mini-bike for Christmas

The reason I want one is that it's a whole new different kind of fun machine.

It's not for riding in the streets and in traffic; you ride it in the dirt or in the country. Like, maybe, if you and I went fishing together, or for a hike, or even just down to some field some Saturday, we could take turns riding it.

We could just put it in the car trunk because the handlebars swing in for easier storing. And the front wheel can be removed too. Either of us can ride it because the seat and handlebars are adjustable.

It's really a neat, great mini-bike. They build it just like the big Suzuki motorcycles— out of reinforced steel; so it'll last a long

time. It has a big headlight; hand-operated front and rear brakes; and an extra-long padded seat. It has front and rear suspension, a louvered muffler guard, and a special tank cover that has 3 racing-style portholes on each side.

It's easy to shift because it's got 3 speeds that work with an automatic clutch. The engine has 3 horsepower; and it's a 2-stroke air cooled job. The gasoline tank holds about a half-gallon, so it would only cost about a quarter to fill it.

And, well, that's why I'd like to have one. Can we talk about this some more? Man-to-Man?

Suzuki Trailhopper: built to take on the country.
U.S. Suzuki Motor Corp., Dept. 1202, 13767 Freeway Dr. Santa Fe Springs, Calif. 90670

Easy Rider

When the easy rider left the highways and took to the trails, the riding wasn't so easy any more.

Then came the Arctic Cat Bikes.

With the easy ride of shock absorber suspension at both ends.

With the easy ride engineered by Arctic Cat's back trail experts.

With the shiftless luxury of automatic transmission.

So now the easy rider is still off the highways, and he's riding easy again.

Quickly, quietly and dependably, too.

Choose one of four models and start riding easy with Arctic Cat Bikes.

Arctic Cat Bikes
Get away from it all. And all the way back.

Capri for 1971.
The first sexy European
under $2400.

There used to be two kinds of imports. Beautiful, sporty and expensive; or plain, dull and inexpensive. Now there's something better than either: it's beautiful and inexpensive. It's Europe's biggest success car in years, and now it's imported for Lincoln-Mercury in limited quantities. Compare it to other imports or new small cars:

Capri offers an extravagant collection of exciting features as standard equipment. Features that are usually optional. Radial tires. Styled steel wheels. Soft vinyl front buckets. Luxurious carpeting. A European-type instrument panel with wood grain effect. Flow-thru ventilation.

Sound unfamiliar for a low-priced car? It is. And there's still more that's standard. Lots of room for four big adults. Easy maintenance (with lots of do-it-yourself tips in the owner's manual). Power disc brakes up front. Four-speed synchromesh transmission. And small car gas economy.

There's only one word for it. Sexy. And that's unheard of at less than $2400. Until now.

Imported for Lincoln-Mercury.

Capri Sport Coupe.

LINCOLN·MERCURY

Lincoln-Mercury Capri, 1970

For 1971, we improved the left side rear window.

At last, a Volkswagen improvement you can see.

Along with our 25 hidden improvements for 1971, we proudly announce a new price.

$1840 will now put you behind the wheel of a Volkswagen 111 sedan.*

You see, we found little things to take out of our little car that won't affect what you get out of it.

(After 25 years of perfecting one model, you can do ingenious things like that.)

For even though it now runs around on a new, more powerful engine, it still runs around on around 26 miles to a gallon.

It still abstains from antifreeze.

It still survives on pints of oil instead of quarts.

 And in case you couldn't tell from the picture above, it still looks like a Beetle.

Volkswagen, 1970

For Spring Only. A Mustang of a New Stripe.

A New Mustang Hardtop. It's a Special Spring Value at your Ford Dealer's. Now.

You take a classic Mustang Hardtop, right? (That practical, comfortable, stylish variety.) Add a sports-car hood—NASA-type scoops and all. Add dual racing mirrors. Color-keyed Spoiler bumper. A unique grille with sport lamps. Brighten the sides with Boss tape stripes. Oh yes, and wide tires with special trim rings. Then take a look at the special prices of the extras. You're home.

Spring won't last forever. Neither will these Special Spring Values at your Ford Dealer's. Now.

MUSTANG (Ford)

The new Toyota Corolla.
Some people find the left rear window
its most beautiful feature.

1798.* That's the beauty mark you'll find on the sticker of every Corolla sedan. But the sedan is just one version of a beautiful Corolla price.

Two other Corollas have left rear windows that are just as appealing. The sporty Corolla Fastback at $1918.* The roomy Corolla Wagon at a mere $1958.*

Yet, as inexpensive as it is, the Toyota Corolla doesn't rely on price alone. It has fully reclining bucket seats. It has

thick wall-to-wall nylon carpeting. It has an all-vinyl interior. To make it all the more beautiful.

But one of the most beautiful surprises in the Toyota Corolla is the amount of legroom. There's not an economy car around that comes close.

As for being practical, the Toyota Corolla does a beautiful job there, too. With carpets that snap in and out so you can clean them easily. With front disc brakes for safer stopping. With undercoating to prevent rust, corrosion and noise. With unit construction and a lined trunk to

prevent rattles and squeaks. And with a very practical sealed lubrication system to end chassis lubes forever.

An economy car that comes loaded. That's the real beauty of the Toyota Corolla.

But with the beautiful price of $1798,* we can't blame you for being attracted to the left rear window.

TOYOTA
We're quality oriented

Finally. A big car as

Have you noticed how everyone's trying to build a small car as good as a Volkswagen?

Well, we think it's time someone built a big car as good as a Volkswagen.

So we did. And there it is.

The 411 Volkswagen 4-Door sedan.

The biggest VW sedan you've ever seen.

And the first VW with four doors.

So now that we've told you what our big surprise is, we'll tell you what it isn't.

The 411 is not a big Beetle.

Because it was built from the ground up to be a different kind of Volkswagen.

With all the comfort and styling of a big car.

And the 411 is not just another big car that eats gas and hogs parking spaces.

So what kind of automobile is it?

It's a big car with plenty of power.

Because we put the most powerful air-cooled engine we've ever built in back.

But it still goes about 22 miles on a gallon.

It's a big car that's as nimble as many small cars. But doesn't need power steering.

It's a big car with plenty of room inside.

Volkswagen 411, 1971

good as a Volkswagen.

But it's only a foot and a half longer than our Beetle outside.

It's a big car with a lot of extras you don't pay extra for:

Like an automatic transmission. Radial tires. Front disc brakes. Reclining bucket seats. Rear-window defogger. Electronic fuel injection. Metallic finish. Undercoating. And more.

Finally, it's a big car just as reliable and sturdy as our little car.

Because since 1965, we've been designing, building and testing the 411 VW 4-Door.

And for the past two years it's been driven millions of miles all over Europe and Africa. Under every road condition imaginable. By thousands of owners.

Now it's here in America.
For only $2999.*

So now, after all these years, you can drive a big car as good as our little car.

 And now everyone else can start all over again.

Trying to build a big car as good as our big car.

The answer
to low cost transportation
is simplicity itself.

Maverick, the original "simple machine," is answering a lot of questions…
   Fewer repair bills? Simple. According to an independent survey, Maverick has the lowest frequency-of-repair record of any American car.
   Better gas mileage? Simple. In simulated city/suburban driving, the standard 100-horsepower-six engine delivers an average of 22 miles per gallon. Less servicing? Simple. One-sixth as many lube jobs and one-half as many oil changes as the leading import. Easier parking? Simple. Maverick has the smallest turning circle of any U.S. compact. Longer life? Simple. Unitized body, deep-down rustproofing and four coats of electrostatically applied paint. And with Maverick, you can choose 2-door, 4-door or sporty Grabber model—with any of three sixes or V-8.
   Any more questions? See the simple machine at your Ford Dealer's.

MAVERICK
The Simple Machine

THE LITTLE CAR THAT GROWS ON YOU.

There are two ways of looking at the Vega Hatchback Coupe.

One, you can look at it as a sporty little 2-seater which, unlike most sporty little 2-seaters, has a back seat you can flip up on those rare occasions when you have three or four people aboard.

Or you can look at it as a sporty little 4-seater which, unlike a lot of sporty little 4-seaters, has a back seat you can flip down when you have a lot of stuff to haul, like on Saturday.

The Vega Hatchback was designed from the outset to be a Hatchback.

It isn't an afterthought.

It is a beautifully balanced, beautifully engineered car with a lot more than just a lot of loadspace to entice you.

There's Vega's surprisingly responsive overhead cam engine, for example. And standard front disc brakes. A double-panel steel roof, side-guard beams in the doors, a 50,000-mile air cleaner, even an electric fuel pump that cuts out to stop the car if the oil pressure ever drops too low.

Vega. It grows on you.

And it's growing on America.

VEGA
CHEVROLET

Ford Maverick, 1971 ◀

Chevrolet Vega Hatchback Coupe, 1971

Mercury's ride rated bette[r] expensive

Official results of blindfold tests show 57 people picked Mercury to 33 fo[r]

The tests were made Jan. 23-29, 1971. 100 people rated Mercury against a $16,000 limousine. Another 100 compared it to a $26,000 European touring car.

The people rating the cars included a cross section of businessmen, teachers, attorneys, engineers, artists, physicians—most of them fine-car owners.

The blindfolds insured objectivity. Cars were identified. Ratings were based solely on smooth[ness], steadiness, quietness and overall ride.

Write for Official Test Report
The complete document detailing test procedures, names of participants and results is available. Write: Nationwide Consumer Testing Institute, P.O. Box 34235, Washington, D.C. 20034.

1. Mercury Marquis starts with a ride that's superior to some of the world's most prestigious cars. That's not just a claim. It's now part of the official record. Tests conducted and certified accurate by the Nationwide Consumer Testing Institute.

2. Then adds the best styling ideas from the luxury class elegantly textured grille set off by concealed headlamps imposing power dome hood. The long unbroken sweep affe[cted] by fender skirts. And the Brougham's chrome-edged vinyl

Mercury Marquis, 1971

BEFORE YOU BUY, DRIVE. BEFORE YOU DRIVE, READ.

Obviously, a motorhome is not something you buy every day.

So, before you do, a little preparation is in order. A thorough test-drive, for example, is a must. And while we admit our motives for recommending one are purely selfish, it's the only true way to appreciate the design features of a GMC Motorhome.

Features like front-wheel drive, tandem rear wheels, and self-leveling air suspension. Mere words can't do such things justice.

But before you take the wheel, we'd like you to read our booklet, "The Pleasures and Delights of the GMC Motorhome." It has answers to a number of fundamental questions you're bound to have about owning a Motorhome. Such as, what's it like to drive? To have serviced? To store? To live in?

And, of course, there's specific information on the GMC itself. Why it's designed and built the way it is. Why it's such a versatile tool for work or play, and so on.

All in all, it's what we hope is an enlightening introduction to a pretty big subject. The booklet won't take long to read. You'll find it as entertaining as it is educational. Best of all, it's free. Why not mail the coupon below now —while you're thinking about it?

 THE MOTOR HOME FROM GENERAL MOTORS

■ COUPON ■

78SSTE

Please send me your book on the pleasures and delights of the GMC Motorhome.

NAME_____

STREET ADDRESS_____

CITY & STATE_____ ZIP_____

Send coupon to: **GMC Motorhome Headquarters**
P.O. Box 3900
Peoria, IL 61614

GM
MARK OF EXCELLENCE

Bob Hope says,
"*Cancel My Reservation,*
I'll take my Apollo."

Bob Hope, star of Naho Enterprises Productions' "Cancel My Reservation," from Warner Bros., always uses his Apollo Motor Home for motion picture locations, mobile office, golf vacations, and cruising enjoyment. Bob says, "Apollo is the only way to go for safety and luxurious accommodations — it gives me all that privacy and Ring-Of-Steel construction."
You need no reservation to see your Apollo dealer for a new experience in first class living

on-the-go. He will be delighted to show you Apollo's exciting, new 1973 line of 22, 25, and 30 foot models in a variety of floor plans and beautiful decorator-coordinated interiors. Features include a bath with sunken tub/shower, sparkling kitchen, and livingroom comfort all contained in a weatherproof, reinforced fiberglass body. Like Bob Hope, drive your Apollo today. For complete information and dealer nearest you, write Apollo Motor Homes, Inc., 9250 Washburn Road, Downey, Calif. 90242.

Select Dealerships available

RING OF STEEL MEANS RING OF SAFETY

APOLLO
MOTOR HOMES
a subsidiary of Kalvex Inc.

Watch Bob Hope Specials on NBC-TV

A man who sees 400 tires a day is a good man to buy a tire from.

Anybody can sell tires. You could sell tires.

But to really know tires, you've got to see all kinds, new and old.

Between tire rotation jobs, fixing flats and just checking tire pressures, an Enco retailer learns a lot.

He learns that the best value you can get is a tire built to stand up under your kind of driving.

Say you need a good-looking tire built for open highway safety and long mileage. He's got it. In a wide-tread tire made to give a firm road grip to today's biggest cars.

Or maybe you want a dependable, low-priced tire for your second car. Your Enco man offers a full four-ply tire in this price range. With a wrap-around tread design that means sure road control.

An Enco retailer will match your driving needs, and your wallet, to the right Atlas tire. Whether it's 4-ply, belted, polyester or nylon cord.

What's more, many Enco retailers are featuring special selling events on Atlas tires and other items for your car.

The right tire, at the right price, right in your neighborhood.

Humble Oil & Refining Company

Trademark "Atlas" Reg. U.S. Pat. Off., Atlas Supply Company.

Trust Texaco Snowmobile Oil
to keep you moving.

When you're out flying over the snowy hills, you want a snowmobile oil you can trust to keep you going.

And Texaco, with 60 years of motor oil experience behind it, has developed a snowmobile oil which is one of the most advanced lubricating and protective oils on the market.

It's designed to protect your motor against spark plug fouling, port-clogging deposits, ring wear, and piston scuffing. What's more, each quart is calibrated for easier mixing, and it's available in convenient 6-bottle, carry-home cartons.

In other words, it's simply smart to use us.

You can trust Texaco to have the right snowmobile oil for you. And out there, that's comforting to know.

TEXACO

We're working to keep your trust.

"THE BEST PUT-TOGETHER CARS OUT OF DETROIT THIS YEAR MAY COME OUT OF WISCONSIN.

AMBASSADOR

Still the only car in its class to offer air-conditioning, V-8 engine, power brakes and automatic transmission as standard equipment.

HORNET

The tough little compact that made a 38,000-mile endurance run throughout North and South America.

GREMLIN

The original American subcompact. Still heavier, wider and more horsepower than any car near its price.

JAVELIN

The car that Mark Donohue and Roger Penske modified to win 7 of 9 Trans-Am races and the 1971 Season Championship.

SPORTABOUT

The only wagon made in America that offers 60.8 cubic feet of cargo space, a rear lift gate, four doors and sleek, racy looks.

MATADOR

The mid-size car chosen for a 500-car fleet by the Los Angeles Police Department on the basis of quality, performance and price.

"Forward Motion" © Peter Max Enterprises, Inc.

New Datsun 1200 Sport Coupe.
An original portrait by Peter Max.

The new Datsun 1200 is today's kind of car. It's an economical package of motion and fun that's nice for you...and for the world around you. So when we commissioned its portrait, we went to today's kind of artist — Peter Max — probably the best known artist of his generation, a creative genius who made colorful visions an exciting part of everyday life.

The new Datsun 1200 Sport Coupe gave him a subject that's exciting on several levels. For the ecology minded, it's a car that doesn't cost much money, doesn't take up much space and gets around 30 miles out of every gallon of gasoline. At the same time it has quick handling and spirited performance. Finally, it comes with all the niceties you could want — fully reclining bucket seats, safety front disc brakes, flow-through ventilation — and a few you didn't expect — a fold-down rear seat storage area, whitewalls and tinted glass, for instance. Peter Max has captured the spirit of our 1200, a Datsun Original. Capture it for yourself in real, everyday terms at your Datsun dealer. Drive a Datsun...then decide.

Own a Datsun Original.
From Nissan with Pride

Cordoba
The Small Chrysler

This is Cordoba. The small Chrysler. An automobile in which you will enjoy
not only great comfort . . . but great confidence. It is confidence you can see, the
confidence of knowing your automobile possesses a look of great dignity.
It is confidence you can *feel*, in thickly cushioned contour-seats available in rich
crushed velour or soft Corinthian leather. It is confidence you experience
when you are in control of a truly road worthy automobile. This is the confidence
you will find in a most surprisingly affordable small Chrysler, Cordoba.

CHRYSLER
MOTORS CORPORATION

Holiday gift ideas from Rolls-Royce.

This is a special holiday season, a season when anyone in the family can give a gift from Rolls-Royce. Gifts that express great affection, imagination, impeccable taste. Gifts with Rolls-Royce eminence, distinction, uniqueness. Gifts you can order through the mail, or

The Corniche Convertible
Lets the sun shine in. A thoroughbred combination of handling, response and power unique to Rolls. Matched veneers from century-old walnuts. The greatest elegance ever borne on a sporting chassis. $38,100.

The Silver Shadow Sedan
The perfect family car, everything in it as good as it could be. Seat leather and exterior/interior finishes by veteran specialists. All the latest motoring advances refined to transcend the feel and function of ordinary luxury sedans. $25,200.

The Corniche Coupé
Expressly for the owner-driver. Strongest of the Rolls-Royces. Coachbuilt by Mulliner, Park Ward. Excellent roofline-to-glass proportions. Four months to build, six weeks alone to paint. The *gran turismo* Rolls that loves to be driven hard. $35,500.

THE '73 OLDS CUTLASS

**The Cutlass S. So much that's new,
it's hard to tell what we didn't change.**

The fastback roof isn't just sportier, it's stronger, too. There's more glass area, thinner corner pillars, improved visibility all around. There's a new ride, patterned after our bigger Oldsmobiles. There's new room inside, and solid-foam seats. (Or you can order a new idea in bucket seats—they swivel.) Yet the Cutlass S is priced within reach of almost any car buyer.

**The Cutlass Supreme. Last year, a little limousine.
This year, a little more limousine.**

Its new formal roofline with opera windows makes it even more distinctive than before. New sound insulation has been added to make it quiet. Its new ride is refined. There's more room —for driver and passengers alike. For extra comfort, a center armrest up front is standard. Yet, with all its luxuries, Cutlass Supreme is trim-sized, easy to handle, and so is its price.

Oldsmobile Cutlass S and Cutlass Supreme, 1972

IT'S TWO NEW CARS.

Just looking, it's easy to tell them apart.
[ther]e's what makes them alike.

The things you expect from Olds. Like a Rocket 350 V8.
[bo]dy by Fisher. The GM safety features. And things you may
[no]t expect. Like instrument panels designed for easy servicing.
[A] new hydraulic front bumper system and a Swing-away grille.

[Is] it any wonder Cutlass S and Supreme are two of America's
[m]ost popular mid-size cars…and outstanding values when trade-
[in] time comes around?   Oldsmobile. Always a step ahead.

'73 Oldsmobile Cutlass:
If your friends could see you now.

Cutlass S Colonnade Hardtop Coupe

Cutlass Supreme Colonnade Hardtop Coupe

"along came SPYDER"
...and blew Miss Muffet's doors off

Miss Muffet and lots of other style conscious dollies go for Spyder guys who get "go" plus "show" running street and strip's hottest newcomer — Spyder wheels. Get Spyder, the trick wheel with muscle • Wide Spyder bite (up to 8" widths) • Spoke aluminum centers • Strong triple plated, chromed steel rims • Precision made for good balance • Meets and beats all automotive strength specifications.

Write: Performance Dept.12129,
Motor Wheel Corp., Lansing, Mich. 48914.

MOTOR WHEEL

That's why they gave her a Subaru.

Subaru. The front wheel drive performer that averages over 27 miles per gallon.
And, to make it almost too good to be true—it's now backed with a strong 12-month
Unlimited Mileage Warranty.
See it and drive it at your local Subaru dealer.

Subaru *Front Drive* **You could buy it for gas mileage alone. But there's so much more**

The Outsiders are doing it all over the country. The long, lean look of power that says it all. Sex symbol?

Sex symbol?

Maybe.

All we know is power It's beautiful.

You can have it for under $100. a set.

Thrush

Thrush Sidepipes, 1972

Appliance Industries Wheels, 1972   ►► *Mercury Cougar, 1971*

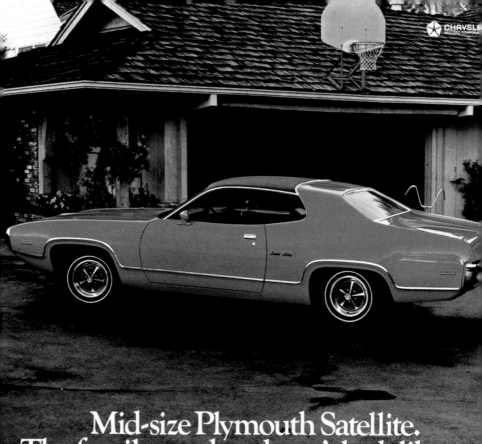

Mid-size Plymouth Satellite.
The family car that doesn't look like on

Despite Satellite's sporty looks, its size and features make it enough car for almost any family.

Satellite gives you plenty of room for six. And we've carved out enough trunk to hold a basket of laundry and a week's worth of groceries.

The standard 318 V-8 means you've got power when you need it for passing or freeway entrances, but it's also easy on your gas budget.

Yet Satellite gives you all this without turning a mid-size car into an over-size car. The wheelbase is only 115 inches. Which means Satellite's maneuverable in city traffic. And easy to park, too.

Another thing you'll appreciate is th way we built Satellite.

We started with a welded Unibody fc strength and tightness. Then we protected this body inside and out with our 7-step dip-and-spray process.

We did a lot of things like this becau we think that's the kind of car America wants. And we're committed to building just that.

Plymouth Satellite. Because we believe a family car should be functional— but not dull.

Coming through with the kind of car America wants.

The 1973 Ford Country Squire.
Now there are more reasons than ever
to make it your next wagon.

Famous 3-Way Doorgate.

Dual facing rear seats.

Load space takes 4 x 8 building panels.

Reclining passenger seat.

Electric rear window defroster.

Power Mini-Vent windows.

One reason more people buy Ford wagons is our wide variety of features. Like the 3-Way Doorgate that opens out for people and down for cargo, and Ford's dual facing rear seats. Now we've added windshield washer jets mounted on the wiper arms. A spare tire extractor. Optional Power Mini-Vent windows. Ford wagons include the full-size Country Squire (above), mid-size Torinos and little Pintos. All with energy-absorbing bumpers and optional steel-belted radial ply tires tested to give the average driver 40,000 miles of tread life with normal driving. At your Ford Dealer.

LTD Country Squire. Standard features include woodgrain bodyside, tailgate treatment, 3-Way Doorgate, automatic transmission, power steering and brakes. Other equipment shown is optional.

When it comes to wagons, nobody swings like Ford.

FORD WAGONS

FORD DIVISION

Determination has its rewards.

A tradition of building great cars like the 1933 Cadillac 355 Phaeton has its advantages—and rewards—for today's luxury car buyer. First, we stubbornly maintain that a luxury car should be a thing of beauty. This is reflected in all nine Cadillacs—including Eldorado, the only American-built luxury convertible. Then, there's Total Cadillac Value. Because of it, Cadillac resale is traditionally the highest of any U.S. luxury car make…and its repeat ownership the greatest of any U.S. car make. Cadillac. **Then and Now…an American Standard for the World.**

Cadillac 🏵 '75

GM
MARK OF EXCELLENCE
Cadillac Motor Car Division

Control and balance make it a beautiful experience

You don't sail a boat just to g
across the water.

The fun is in the doing.

The pleasure of motion unde
control.

Mustang drivers understand
If all they wanted was to get fr
here to there, they'd be driving
something else. Not a Ford Mu

With independent front sus
sion and an anti-sway bar to gi
you good control, good road
handling.

With bucket seats to positio
comfortably behind the wheel.

With a cockpit design and fl
mounted shift that give you a
beautiful feeling the instant y
inside.

There are five sporty Musta
models: Hardtop, SportsRoof,
Convertible, Mach 1, Grande.
And a selection of five engines
three transmissions. What it
takes to make driving a beauti
experience is what Ford pu
into Mustang.

1972 Mustang Mach 1

FORD MUSTA

FORD DIVISION

We've come a long way from basic black.

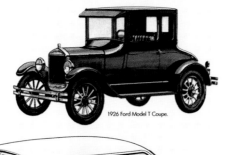

1926 Ford Model T Coupe.

1972 Ford Pinto Runabout with Sprint Decor Option.

If you find yourself staring whenever you see a Model "T" go by, we don't blame you. It was some kind of car. (Even if it did come mostly in black.) It was simple. It was tough. And if something went wrong, you could probably fix it with a screwdriver and a pair of pliers.

Pinto has many of those same qualities. Which is good to know if you're the kind of person who likes cars, and likes to work on them. Pinto is the kind of car you <u>can</u> work on, without having to be some kind of master mechanic. It's also a car you can work with. There are lots of things you can add—both from Pinto's list of options and from the specialty equipment people. If you start with the Sprint Option we've shown, you don't even have to start with basic black.

Sprint Decor Group includes the following equipment: Red, White and Blue Exterior Accents. Trim Rings with Color-Keyed Hubcaps. Dual Racing Mirrors. Red, White and Blue Cloth and Vinyl Bucket Seats. Full Carpeting. Deluxe 2-Spoke Steering Wheel. Stars and Stripes Decal. A78 x 13 White Sidewall Tires. Blackout Grille.

When you get back to basics, you get back to Ford.

FORD PINTO

FORD DIVISION

Better idea for safety...buckle up!

Anatomy of a Gremlin

1. Gremlin is the only little economy car with a standard 6-cylinder engine.

2. Reaches turnpike speed easily.

3. Weighs more than other small cars. And its wheels are set wider apart.

4. Has a wider front seat.

5. A wider back seat.

6. And more headroom in the trun[k]

And only American Motors makes thi[s] promise: The Buyer Protection Plan back[s] every '73 car we build. And we'll see that ou[r] dealers back that promise.

1. 2. 3. 4. 5. 6.

Buckle up for safe[ty]

AMC Gremlin

We back them better because we build them better.

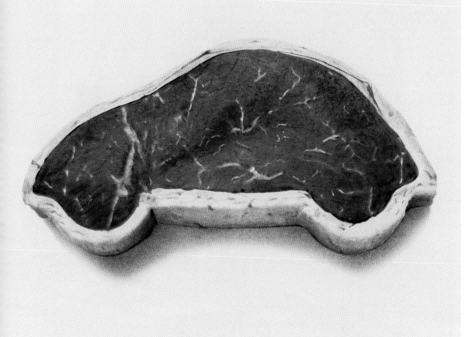

© VOLKSWAGEN OF AMERICA, INC.

Can you still get prime quality for $1.26 a pound?

A pound of Volkswagen isn't cheap compared to other cars. But what you pay for is the quality. Prime quality.

Just look at what you get for your money:

13 pounds of paint, some of it in places you can't even see. (So you can leave a Volkswagen out overnight and it won't spoil.)

A watertight, airtight, sealed steel bottom that protects against rocks,

*DIN 70030

rain, rust and rot.

Over 1,000 inspections per one Beetle.

1,014 inspectors who are so finicky that they reject parts you could easily ride around with and not even detect there was anything wrong.

Electronic Diagnosis that tells you what's right and wrong with important parts of your car.

A 1600 cc aluminum-magnesium engine that gets 25* miles to a gallon

of regular gasoline.

Volkswagen's traditionally high resale value.

Over 22,000 changes and improvements on a car that was well built to begin with.

What with all the care we take in building every single Volkswagen, we'd like to call it a filet mignon of a car. Only one problem. It's too tough.

Few things in life work as well as a Volkswagen.

The best Germany, England, Italy and America have to offer.

Some of the finest cars in the world are made in the aforementioned countries.

And some of the finest features of those cars are found in one car: The Audi.

For example, Germany's most luxurious automobile is, without question, the Mercedes-Benz. And her "Beste" sportscar is the Porsche.

Well, it just so happens that the Audi's interior bears an uncanny resemblance to the Mercedes-Benz 280SE's. And her ignition system is the same type as the Porsche 911's.

England's stately and dignified King is the Rolls-Royce. And her regal sportscar is the Aston Martin.

the same as the Silver Shadow's. And her independent front suspension is like the Aston's.

Italy's "Numero Uno" is the Ferrari. The Audi's steering system is the same type as the racing Ferrari.

And America's two greats are the Cadillac Eldorado and the Lincoln Continental Mark IV. The Audi has front-wheel drive like the Cadillac and the same trunk space as the Lincoln.

Isn't it nice to know you can ride with English dignity, German precision, Italian flair and American practicality?

The $4,385* Audi

You may never need all 120 safety features in your Mercedes-Benz. But it's comforting to know they're there.

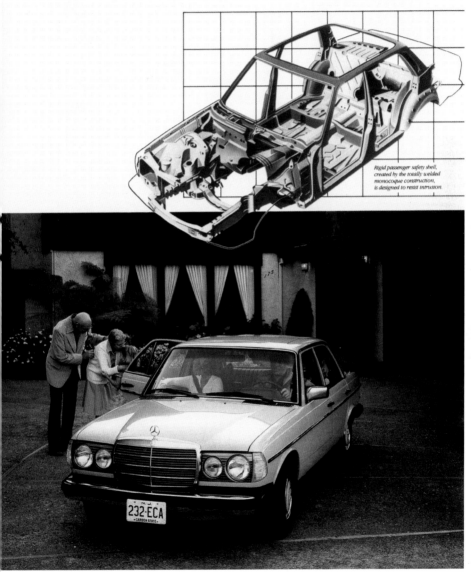

Rigid passenger safety shell, created by the totally welded monocoque construction, is designed to resist intrusion.

How to tell a Mercedes-Benz 450SEL from all the rest.

450 SEL

CONTEMPORARY VERSION OF CLASSIC TOURING CAR: TRIM EXTERIOR SIZE, UNUSUALLY GENEROUS INTERIOR ROOM. A LIMITED EDITION AUTOMOBILE.

56.3"

59.9"
73.6"

UNIQUE ENGINE: 8 CYLINDERS, V-TYPE, OVERHEAD CAMSHAFT. BREAKERLESS TRANSISTORIZED IGNITION. C.I.S. MECHANICALLY-OPERATED FUEL INJECTION. ELECTRIC FUEL PUMP. FORGED STEEL CRANKSHAFT. SODIUM FILLED EXHAUST VALVES. LIGHT ALLOY CYLINDER HEAD.

CONTROL PANEL.
- ADJUSTABLE AIR VENTS.
- AUTOMATIC CLIMATE CONTROL.
- AM/FM STEREO RADIO WITH ADJUSTABLE ELECTRIC ANTENNA.
- ELECTRICALLY OPERATED WINDOWS.

- 3-SPEED AUTOMATIC TRANSMISSION WITH TORQUE CONVERTER.
- FULL INSTRUMENTATIO[N] PLUS TACHOMETER.
- CRUISE CONTROL.

POWER STEERING: RECIRCULATING BALL-TYPE. TURNING CIRCLE: 39'. TELESCOPIC STEERING COLUMN. ADDITIONAL SHOCK ABSORBER DAMPENS ROAD VIBRATIONS.

STEERING GEAR CASE: LOCATED BEHIND FRONT AXLE FOR SAFETY.

COLLAPSIBLE EXTREMITIES RIGID PASSENGER SHELL.

GAS TANK: MOUNTED OVER REAR AXLE, 45 INCHES IN FROM REAR BUMPER AND SURROUNDED BY STEEL BULKHEADS

SAFETY BUMPERS: RUBBER PROTECTED WITH HYDRAULIC REGENERATIVE SHOCK ABSORBERS.

34.4" 38.6"
37.1"
19.6" 19.4"
58.1"

116.7"
209.4"

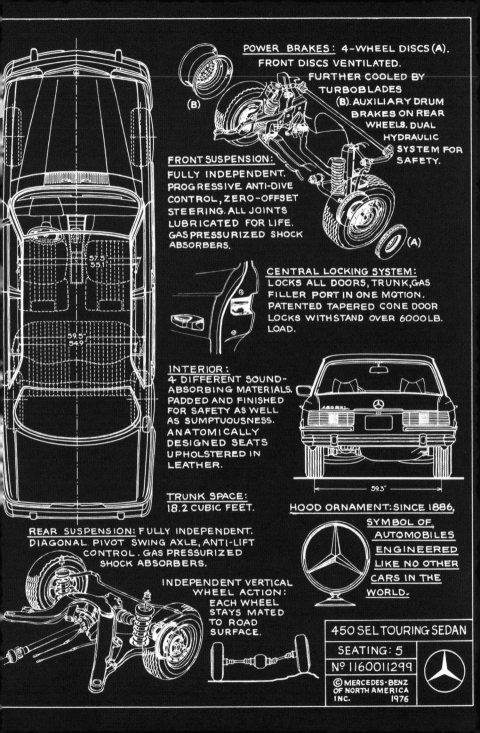

We have a very strong respect for other people's money.

The 1972 mid-size Ford Torino is very strong proof of it.

The new Torino now has a rugged body/frame construction like our quiet Ford LTD.

And a tough new rear suspension.

Torino's even built a little heavier and a little wider this year.

It's so solid on the road, steady on the curves and smooth on the bumps, we've been calling it the "Easy Handler."

Torino's even bigger inside.

With Torino's standard front disc brakes, you *stop*. Really Stop!

And you'll like the reassuringly positive feel of Torino's new integral power steering. (It's optional.)

And Ford did all this to make Torino a better value for you...quite possibly more car than you expected.

And quiet because it's a Ford.

Find out at your local Ford Dealer's.

Gran Torino Hardtop. One of 9 new models. Bucket seat interior, vinyl roof, wheel trim rings and white sidewall tires are optional.

More car than you expected.

FORD TORINO

FORD DIVISION

1974 MERCURY COUGAR XR-7

QUALITY.

Quality in a small car. What does this mean to you? To Toyota it means an automobile that's inexpensive, not cheap. The new generation of Toyota Corollas are built with quality. The proof? 9 out of 10 Toyota cars sold in this country since 1958 are still on the road today. Quality. You asked for it. You got it. Toyota.

Quality is durability and how a car handles the road. Power assisted front disc brakes help you maintain control. MacPherson strut front suspension helps keep the ride smooth and unit body welded construction helps keep the Corolla tight and virtually rattle free.

Toyota's quality is in a line, not one car. No matter what your space needs you'll find it in one of ten Corollas: the Hardtop, 2-Door Sedan, 2- or 4-Door Deluxe Sedan, 5-Door Wagon, the new Sport Coupe or the new Liftback™ with a split, fold down rear seat. And there's a sporty equipped SR-5 model of the Hardtop, Sport Coupe and Liftback.

A quality car can be economical. The Toyota Corolla gets great gas mileage. Note: 1976 EPA tests, with 5-speed overdrive transmission, 39 mpg on highway, 24 city. These EPA results are estimates. The actual mileage you get will vary depending on your driving habits and your car's condition and equipment. California EPA ratings will differ. An automatic transmission is available on Deluxe models.

YOU ASKED FOR IT.

Quality. You asked for it. You got it at nearly 1,000 authorized dealers across the U.S. These same dealers comprise a network of service departments with Toyota trained mechanics. The new generation of Toyota Corollas. If you can find a better built small car than a Toyota,...buy it.

39 MPG HIWAY / 24 CITY

YOU GOT IT.

Corolla SR-5 Sport Coupe

Corolla SR-5 Liftback.

A NEW GENERATION OF TOYOTA COROLLAS

"Women only drive automatic transmissions."

Some car manufacturers actually believe women buy cars for different reasons than men do.

So they build "a woman's car." Oversized, hopelessly automatic and dull.

At Honda we designed just one thing. A lean, spunky economy car with so much pizzazz it handles like a sports car.

If you're bored with cars designed only to get you from point A to point B, without responding to you the driver, maybe you ought to take the Honda Civic for a spin.

We've got a stick shift with an astonishing amount of zip. Enough to surprise you. We promise.

Or, if you prefer, Hondamatic.™ It's a semi-automatic transmission that gives you convenience, but doesn't rob you of involvement.

Neither one is a woman's car.

Honda Civic.
We don't make "a woman's car."

© 1974 American Honda Motor Co., Inc.

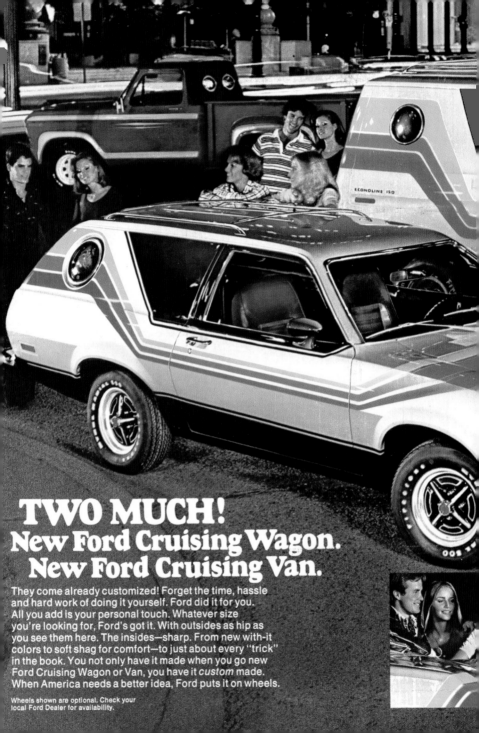

TWO MUCH!
New Ford Cruising Wagon.
New Ford Cruising Van.

They come already customized! Forget the time, hassle and hard work of doing it yourself. Ford did it for you. All you add is your personal touch. Whatever size you're looking for, Ford's got it. With outsides as hip as you see them here. The insides—sharp. From new with-it colors to soft shag for comfort—to just about every "trick" in the book. You not only have it made when you go new Ford Cruising Wagon or Van, you have it *custom* made. When America needs a better idea, Ford puts it on wheels.

Wheels shown are optional. Check your
local Ford Dealer for availability.

Cruising Van.

Inside and out—it's ready to roll. Mag-style wheel covers, shag carpeting over entire cargo area, including floor, walls, ceiling, side and rear. Plus! Porthole windows, spare tire and cover, and roof rack. The Industry's first Factory-built completely customized van!

Pinto Cruising Wagon.

Part wagon, part van, all fun. Ford's restyled Pinto wagon up front, wide open van room in rear. Has bubbled porthole windows, front spoiler, dual racing mirrors, styled steel wheels with trim rings, and sports rallye package. An Industry exclusive! Choose from many color and tape stripe combinations.

Wild wagon stuff!

A super interior. Stylish and comfortable. A roomy wagon combined with the class and kicks of the hot Van look.

Captain's Chairs for easy livin'.

Great way to ride 'n relax. Swivel to rap, or turn easily to the back. Fold-down arm rests, too.

Along came a Spyder.

"You can tell as soon as you key the engine to life. There's a
thump to the exhaust, a resonance . . . the hammer-heavy beat of a V8 that's
taking care of business . . ." *Car and Driver*, September, 1976.
 Meet Spyder. We had to build it. There were too many of you out
there who refused to forget that performance is more than
pinstripes and fancy wheel covers.
 So along comes Spyder, an honest, gutty car from Chevy that
lives up to its looks. It's not for everybody. But if you've read this far and the
velvet beat of a V8 is playing tunes in your head, then it's for you.

MONZA SPYDER

Chevrolet

Chevrolet Monza Spyder, 1976

Action is having an electronic fuel-injected 2.0-liter engine take you from 0 to 60 in 11.0 seconds.

Action is stopping on radial tires with 4-wheel disc brakes.

Action is taking a corner with rack–and-pinion steering in a mid-engine car and feeling closer to the road than the white line.

The Action

Action is a 5-speed gearbox.

Action is a light, fiberglass roof you can take off in less than a minute.

Action is sporting a built-in roll bar.

Action is 13 of the wildest colors you've ever seen. From Zambezi Green to Signal Orange.

Action is 29 miles to the gal-

lon and a cruising range of more than 400 miles on one tank of gas.

Action is finally stopping for gas and having all the station attendants wanting to wait on you.

Action is what you get every time you step into a mid-engine Porsche 914.

Porsche

Targa. The revolutionary roof design by
Porsche that has become almost as famous as the car itself. Giving all the fun
and freedom of the old "convertible"
with the structural integrity of a
built-in roll bar. Plus a sturdy
year-round roof that's off
and in the trunk in sec-
onds. So whether it's
the handcrafted,
superbly engi-
neered 911, or the
thrilling mid-engine
914 2.0, you're assured
of unique Porsche han-
dling, unique Porsche
styling, and a breath of
fresh air when you want it.
For that there is no substitute.

PORSCHE
THERE IS NO SUBSTITUTE

Porsche Targa, 1974

It puts the driving back in driving.

There are two kinds of driving. One is the kind you do in
Monza Towne Coupe and the other isn't. You'll know the difference.
Driving a Monza Towne Coupe puts you on the same team
as the road. And there's an excitement to that kind of driving
that you'll like.
The Monza's not short on available equipment, either. There
re sky roofs; Positraction rear axle; a special suspension package;
port equipment and sport front end (pictured here) with finned wheel
overs, quad headlights, some spiffy upholstery combinations
nd a lot more.
And its styling is something to see. Styling that says a lot
bout Monza's character. And yours.

MONZA

TOWNE COUPE

Chevrolet

Chevrolet Monza Towne Coupe, 1976 ►► *Porsche + Audi, 1977*

COME IN AND DR

"Legend." That's a pretty strong word, isn't it?

Though we sincerely doubt anyone would consider it too strong whe referring to Porsche. After having become possibly the foremost name in racing. After almost thirty years of major automotive innovations not only the track but on the road. Culminating in the Porsche Turbo Carrera, a car with such painstaking pride and to such exacting standards that it takes twelve days to build one.

And Audi's credentials are equally impressive.

You probably didn't know it, but Audi has a history that dates all the w

The 1977 AUDI

Our $5445* Audi Fox Sedan with new aerodynamic front-end design and fuel-injected engine w propels the car from 0 to 50 in 8 seconds yet delivers EPA estimated 36 mpg on the highway and the city for standard shift model (mileage may vary with driver, car's condition and equipm *Suggested 1977 retail price, P.O.E. Transportation, local taxes, and dealer delivery charges, additi Whitewalls optional.

ONE OF OUR LEGENDS.

back to 1904 (that's before the Model T). A history that includes a succession of accomplishments on the track <u>and</u> on the road. (Would you believe back in the 30s we had such advanced features as front-wheel drive and dual braking systems?)

But more important than any specific feature of either car is a dedication to engineering excellence and innovation that has been a hallmark of Porsches and Audis through the years. That has separated them from other cars. That has made them more than just...cars.

PORSCHE +AUDI

The 1977 PORSCHE

Our $28,000* Porsche Turbo Carrera: Not only the fastest production car Porsche ever built (0 to 60 in less than 6 seconds) but the most luxurious (supple leather seats, deep-cut pile carpeting, automatic temperature control, even 4-speaker stereo). *Suggested 1977 retail price, P.O.E. Transportation, local taxes, and dealer delivery charges additional.

SIMPLY BEAUTIFUL

The New Lotus Esprit
Colin Chapman's latest, exotic, 2-litre, mid-engine, two-seat, high performance sports car incorporates all the best features of the racing car that has won more Formula One Grands Prix than any of its competitors including the 1977 U.S. Grand Prix West. Lotus Esprit is designed for style, comfort, performance, safety and beauty.

Manufacturer's suggested list price under $17,000.*

5-speed manual transmission, GFRP body, rack & pinion steering
9.7 ins disc front/10.6 ins rear (rear inboard)
height: 43.75″ width: 73.25″ length: 165″ wheelbase: 96″
front track: 59.5″ rear track: 59.5″ ground clearance: 5.5″
boot capacity: 7.0 cu. ft. weight (kerb): 1980 lbs.
California EPA 29 MPG Highway. 17 MPG City. The actual mileage you get will vary depending on the type of driving you do, your driving habits, your car's condition, and optional equipment.

esprit

Doug's Lynwood Dodge & Lotus—Lynwood Wash.; H & K Development Co., Ltd. Inc.—Reno, Nev.; Jamestown Motor Center—Long Beach, Cal.; Jim Loose Imported Cars—Palo Alto, Cal.; Los Gatos Motors—Los Gatos, Cal.; Love-Thomas Motors—Honolulu, Hawaii; Luff Motor Company—Salt Lake City, Utah; Manhattan Beach Imported Cars, Inc.—Manhattan Beach, Cal.; R.D. Nesen Cadillac-Oldsmobile—Thousand Oaks, Cal.; Ramsay McCue Imported Cars—San Bernardino, Cal.; Santa Monica Imported Cars—Santa Monica, Cal.; Southwest Motor Car Company—Beverly Hills, Cal.; Sunnyslope Car Company—Phoenix, Ariz.; Don Sutton Motors—San Francisco, Cal.; Ventura Datsun—Ventura, Cal.; Wester Porsche Audi—Seaside, Cal.; Mission Viejo Imports—Mission Viejo, Cal.; Pierres Motors of Portland, Ltd.—Portland, Ore.

*West Coast P.O.E. subject to change and availability
See James Bond's Lotus Esprit Submarine Car at Auto Expo April 29-May 8.

here's a Firebird for every purpose.
Except standing still.

orit offers luxury that doesn't in the way of sport. Individually-hioned buckets of supple vinyl. osewood-vinyl accented dash. sh cut-pile carpet underfoot. Plus available "Sky Bird" Package h sky blue paint, matching eels and special trim throughout.

Formula Firebird is for people o are driven by a love of driving. ho are forever inspired by dual

simulated air scoops atop a 5.0 litre V-8. Who can appreciate stabilizer bars and steel-belted radials.

Trans Am is the ultimate Firebird. Built to go all the way. An eye-catching, head-turning, heart-wrenching, awe-inspiring legend.

A lot of it has to do with the ominous air extractors, deflectors and air dam. The shrieking bird available for the hood. And the

6.6 litre V-8 underneath.

Even the base Firebird has a purpose. To deliver Firebird's fire at an appealing price.

Firebirds are equipped with GM-built engines produced by various divisions. Your dealer has details. He also has a Firebird for whatever you like to do.

Unless you like standing still.

Pontiac ▼ The Mark of Great Cars

1978 ▼ Pontiac's best year yet!

Porsche Targa, 1973

"That's IT"

Just as a great painting is more than canvas and paints, there are some things that go beyond the sum of their parts. The Porsche Targa is such an object.

It is a piece of machinery whose purpose far exceeds transporting you from one point to another. The Targa's goal is to afford the ultimate driving experience. In performance, in engineering, in comfort.

The Targa has come amazingly close to that goal; each year, subtle improvements, a bit m

First, consider its supe thought-out features. It ha built-in roll bar, and a huge rear window. To give the ca practicality of a hardtop co And you the exhilarating ex ence of a roadster.

It has an aerodynamic sh

protect you from wind blast.
d a rear-engine design that has
n steadily improved upon for
years.
All controls are meticulously
ineered to be functional and
ically accessible.
Yet it is the total effect of these
ovations that impresses.
With the removable top stored

in the trunk, cushioned in luxurious bucket seats, you ride in
"Belle Epoque" comfort.

But the grandest feature of the
Targa is the experience of driving it.

The handling is quick, correct,
precise, because of Porsche's leg-
endary engineering. Putting the
driver and car in perfect collab-

oration. It is almost as if you just
"think" where you want the car to
go.

The Targa is available in all
three 911 models: 911T, 911E,
and 911S.

But be warned.

It is very difficult to be humble
about owning any Porsche. And
if it's a Targa, that's IT.

Rolls-Royce brings back a great name. Silver Wraith II.

The last of the Silver Wraiths was built in 1959. Or so it seemed at the time.

But the richest of Rolls-Royce memories have a way of living on in the newest of Rolls-Royce motor cars. And so it is with the Silver Wraith II of 1977.

The Timeless Pleasure

The long, sleek look of the Silver Wraith II reflects a time gone by.

You can sense it in the graceful lines, the contrasting top, the gleaming bright work, the tasteful craftsmanship and the roomy interior.

And, for the most up-to-date reasons, the Silver Wraith II is a new air of comfort, a new sense of quiet and a new feeling of command.

A new rack-and-pinion steering system makes the Silver Wraith II quick to respond and rewarding to drive, no matter how narrow the road or sudden the curve.

A unique automatic air-conditioning system maintains any temperature you desire at two levels of the interior. And, because the system creates a rarefied atmosphere all your own, its built-in sensors alert you to outside temperatures as well as icy roads.

The Silver Wraith II also offers you the sophistication of an advanced electrical system, the performance of a quiet V-8 engine, the security of a dual braking system and the sensitivity of a self-leveling suspension.

And, to name one of the many other subtle details you'll discover, the electronic odometer will contemplate recording the miles from 000000.0 to 999999.9.

The Priceless Asset

From the distinctive radiator grille to the matching walnut veneers, the Silver Wraith II is built almost entirely by hand.

In tribute to this enduring Rolls-Royce tradition, it is no coincidence that more than half of all the motor cars we have ever built remain very much on the road.

And, in return for the purchase price of $49,000,* it is little wonder that a Silver Wraith II speaks so warmly of the past and so surely of the future.

‹‹‹ ‹‹‹ ‹‹‹

A collection of Rolls-Royce masterpieces is waiting at your nearest Authorized Rolls-Royce Dealership. For further information, call 800-325-6000 and give this ID number: 1000.

*Suggested U.S. Retail Price March 1, 1977. The names "Rolls-Royce" and "Silver Wraith" and the mascot, badge and radiator grille are all Rolls-Royce trademarks.
© Rolls-Royce Motors Inc. 1977.

The heart and soul of a masterpiece

The Answer to Exclusivity

Combine the General Motors drive line with EXCALIBUR'S body and frame, and you have the nostalgia of yesterday with the dependability and comfort of today. EXCALIBUR, manufacturing fine motor cars since 1964 for people who thought they had everything.

EXCALIBUR SALES, INC.
Milwaukee, WI
(414) 771-8240

EXCALIBUR SOUTHWEST, INC.
Houston, TX
(713) 691-1703

EXCALIBUR WEST, INC.
Reno, NV
(702) 323-2758

This is the new 1979 Lincoln Versailles.

This is the new 1979 Lincoln Versailles.

Valino grain roof

This is the new 1979 Lincoln Versailles.
The pride of owning a Lincoln distilled to a 110-inch wheelbase. Your choice of
custom roof designs makes the new Versailles a most personal luxury car.

LINCOLN VERSAILLES
LINCOLN-MERCURY DIVISION

The daily routine. Hurried. Harried. On the run. Wouldn't it be nice to have an Escape Machine?

1970 Olds Delta 88 Royale, Youngmobile Thinking opens up the big-car world.

A nice place to be, the big-car world of Oldsmobile. Roomy. Relaxing. Very, very elegant. Turn the key on this Delta 88 Royale and a Rocket 455 V-8 comes on strong in the performance department. And stays strong—delivers smoother, longer lasting V-8 performance—thanks to a new Oldsmobile exclusive: Positive Valve Rotators. What do they do for you? They rotate the valves constantly—providing better valve seating and perfect sealing for longer, more efficient engine operation. Also standard on Royale: vinyl top, fender louvers, pinstriping. But there are a number of nice things you can't even see on a Delta 88. Like a radio antenna cleverly concealed in the windshield glass—nothing to mar those sleek lines. And body sideguard beams—extra protection built right into the doors. You can even order a washer/wiper control conveniently built into the gear selector lever. Try an Olds Escape Machine today.

Oldsmobile: Escape from the ordinary.

Protects you with energy-absorbing padded instrument panel, sideguard beams, bias-ply glass-belted tires, side marker lights and reflectors, four-way hazard warning flasher, anti-theft steering column. **Pampers you** with luxurious interiors, rotary glove box latch, easy-to-read instruments. **Pleases you** with Oldsmobile's famous quiet ride, responsive power, and contemporary styling. Come see it soon.

Lincoln Versailles, 1978 ◄   *Oldsmobile Delta 88 Royale, 1970*

Cadillac  presents the class of '73.

The class. The style. And the gra[...]
Clearly, these are the most magnificent ca[...]
Cadillac has ever built. Not only for what you ca[...]
see—the bold new exteriors and the plush ne[...]
interiors—but as much for what you can't s[...]
You see here the sparkling new Sedan deVille, th[...]
stunning new Eldorado Coupe and the superb ne[...]
Eldorado Convertible. You don't see the six oth[...]

Cadillac, 1972

1973

…ew Cadillacs (more models than all the other U.S. luxury cars have combined).

You see here the striking new styling outside—simpler, bolder, even more elegant for '73. You don't see the myriad innovations and refinements inside. To add new comfort and convenience. To make that great Cadillac ride even smoother. To make Cadillac's lasting value even more lasting.

And you don't see the new niceties you may add. Like a lighted vanity mirror for the lady. An outside thermometer. A lap robe and pillow. As well as a theft-deterrent system and steel-belted radial tires. In the Brougham, crushed velour interiors in beige, blue, maize or taupe. Clearly, you never had so many good reasons to visit your authorized Cadillac dealer. Cadillac Motor Car Division. The leadership shows.

INTRODUCING A WOLF IN WOLF'S CLOTHING.

It comes dressed in special paint, a sleek teardrop tank, flashy megaphone pipes, and lots of chrome. All the markings of a bigger beast.

And like its big brothers, it's ridden in a more natural, laid-back position. With a low-riding stepped seat. And handlebars that reach back for you instead of the other way around.

But our XS400 has more than the profile. It has the power.

In fact, *Cycle Guide* magazine found that it's the fastest accelerating four-stroke 400 you can buy. And one of the best handling motorcycles anywhere.

Or, as they put it, "the only limit to how much fun you have is how much lean angle you like."

How did all this come about? Engineering.

For example, the suspension system not only gives you big bike steadiness, but it can be fine tuned for any rider, any riding style.

And the carburetors automatically adjust to engine load. So there's a lot of power, but not a lot of temperment.

Plus there are features like an overhead cam, electric starting, 6-speed transmission, self-cancelling turn signals, disc brakes, and

complete instrumentation that's angled back for easier reading.

There's even an economy model, the XS400-2F, for those of you on a little tighter budget. It has wire wheels instead of ca alloy, slightly less chrome, a kic starter, drum brakes. And it com in one color instead of two. In a other respects, it's identical to our regular model.

Which means it does a who lot more than look like a bigger bike.

It acts like one.

YAMAHA
When you know how they're bu

F

Obviously, it's a
Fox. Plush velour
upholstery, cut-pile
carpeting, and
fully reclining bucket
seats. It's rich. It
looks it. It knows it.

A Fox? No question.
It goes 0 to 50 mph
in a wild 8.1 seconds.
From front bumper
to back, it's all
brain and muscle.
No fat. It's Fox.

Indeed it is a Fox.
Surefooted in traffic,
spirited on the open
road. You know a
Fox when you see
one. You sense a Fox
when it responds.

O

Of course, it's a Fox.
In rough road or
weather conditions,
the engine over the
drive wheels gives
you the traction
to get out and away.

Naturally, it's a Fox.
From front-wheel
drive to rack-and-
pinion steering to ra-
dial tires, it has good
reason to be secure
in its environment.

True Fox. 37 mpg
hwy. 23 city; std. shift.
(EPA Est. Actual mile-
age may vary based
on how and where
you drive, car's con-
dition, optional equip.)

BY
X
AUDI

Le City Car

One of the reasons Le Car has caused so much excitement in this country is because of what it can do in the city. There isn't a car in town that can match Le Car for parking, maneuverability, ease of handling and smooth ride.

Le Car fits in a smaller parking space than any other car in its class.

Even though Le Car has a longer wheelbase than Honda Civic or VW Rabbit, it has a shorter overall length. So Le Car will fit in a space

that the others have to pass by. Add to this Le Car's short 32-foot turning circle and you can see why the parking problems of the city are no problem for Le Car.

A highly responsive car that handles with ease.

Parking is not the only difficulty you'll encounter in the city. Driving is another. Le Car is equipped with front-wheel drive, rack and pinion steering, four-wheel independent suspension and Michelin steel-belted radials, all standard. (Honda, Rabbit, Chevette and Fiesta don't offer this combination of standard features.) The result is that Le Car can zip in and out of, around and through traffic.

And Le Car's ride is so remarkably smooth that Car & Driver reported, "The rough-road ride in Le Car is a new standard for small cars. It waltzed across the worst roads we could find—the cratered surfaces of Manhattan—as though it was fresh pavement."

Although Le Car is small on the

outside you could never tell from its roomy inside. Le Car is designed to give you the most interior room while using the least exterior space.

A world of satisfied Le Car owners.

In Europe, nearly two million people drive Le Car with a passion. That's more than Fiesta and Rabbit combined. Here in America, Le Car sales more than doubled in 1977. What's more, in an independent study, Le Car owner satisfaction was rated an amazingly high 95%. The price for all this? A very satisfying $3495.*

Obviously, a lot of people are doing a lot more than just driving Le Car in the city. So if you really want to see how much fun Le Car can be, flip open the giant sun roof (optional) and take Le City Car for a drive in the country. For more information call 800-631-1616 for your nearest dealer. In New Jersey call collect 201-461-6000.

*P.O.E. East Coast: Price excludes transportation, dealer preparation and taxes. Stripe, Mag wheels, Sun roof and Rear wiper/washer optional at extra cost. Prices higher in the West. Renault USA, Inc. ©1978.

Le Car by Renault ◈

FIESTA

FORD FIESTA
FORD DIVISION

Ford

75ᵗʰ ANNIVERSARY

1979 RABBIT. THE CAR EVERYBODY'S TRYING TO COPY.

No wonder.

How often does a car cor along with the Rabbit's com nation of engineering, perf mance, space and handling

And when you realize th even General Motors nam our Rabbit the best of fi economy cars tested, inclu ing one of their own, it's r surprising that the Rab became the best-selling i port in Detroit.

So you can't blam people for trying to ma their cars look like ours.

But to look like a Rab

Volkswagen Rabbit, 1978

ot to be a Rabbit.

he Rabbit is available with a
S. fuel-injected engine. The
pies aren't.

lot all the copies match our
bbit's room. For example, the
d Fiesta has only 2/3 as
ch trunk space as the Rab-
. As a matter of fact, the
bbit has more trunk space
n a $90,000 Rolls. And more
ssenger space than 35 other
s on the market.

nd after testing the 13 most
oular '78 economy cars in
erica, here's what the
tors of <u>Car and Driver</u> had to

say: "The Rabbit's total design
is more astute than that of any
other car in this test ... And
painstaking year-to-year re-
finement has made the Rabbit
good at everything it does."

Of course, this excellence
has a price. The Rabbit costs
slightly more than its imitators.
But as the editors so aptly put it,
"...the Rabbit delivers on the
investment."

Four years ago, other car
manufacturers bought our
Rabbits by the dozens. Then
took them apart to see how we
did it. Now we're beginning to

see the fruits of that labor.

One of these days, they may
even get it right.

VOLKSWAGEN DOES IT AGAIN

MG Midget.
High-flying fun.
Low-flying pricetag.

In the wide-open MG Midget, you can fly now, pay little, and even save money on gas while enjoying all the fun of owning a real, live, top-down sports car while you're still young enough to enjoy it.

The Midget is, in fact, the lowest-priced true sports car on the market.

The Midget has rack and pinion steering, short-throw four-speed stick, front disc brakes and an agility in turns and a feel for the road that make it a joy to handle. Not to mention an impressive EPA-rated 34 MPG on the highway and 22 MPG in the city. (Naturally, these are estimates and the actual mileage you get may vary depending on the car's condition and how and where you drive, optional equipment, and may be lower in California.)

If whatever you're driving is getting you down, go fly a Midget. It's fun. It's inexpensive. It's thrifty to run. For the name of the dealer nearest you, call these numbers toll-free: (800) 447-4700, or, in Illinois, (800) 322-4400.

British Leyland Motors Inc., Leonia, New Jersey 07605.

JAGUAR

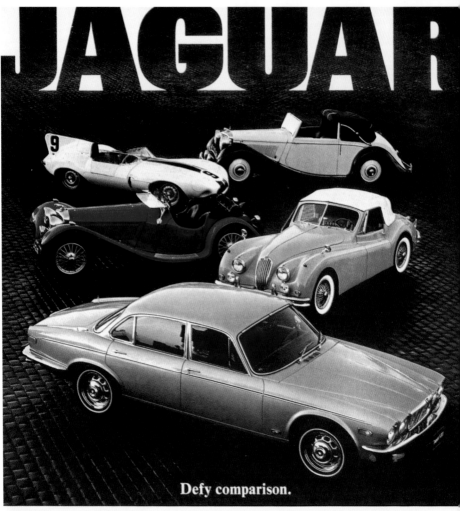

Defy comparison.

Jaguars have always been defiantly individual cars. Consider the XJ12; it is literally a class of one, the only production four-door V-12 sedan in the world. And this uncompromising machine is unique in ways that extend far beyond its source of power.

The XJ12 handles with the agility and precision of all-independent suspension, rack and pinion steering and power disc brakes on all four wheels. The great smoothness and response of the electronically fuel-injected V-12 only enhance the car's remarkable all-round performance characteristics.

The inner world of this uncommon sedan is a harmony of thoughtful luxuries: hand-matched walnut veneers enrich the dashboard. Topgrain hides cover the seats. The car is totally considerate of its occupant's every wish: there are no factory options whatever. Even the thermostatically-controlled heat and air conditioning and the AM/FM stereo radio and tape deck are standard.

Still another Jaguar amenity is a remarkably thoughtful warranty: for 12 months, regardless of mileage, Jaguar will replace or repair any part of the car that is defective or that simply wears out, provided only that the car is properly maintained.

The only exceptions are the tires, which are warranted by the tire manufacturer, and spark plugs and filters, which are routine replacement items. Even then, if the plugs or filters are defective, Jaguar will pay to replace them.

In a world filled with common denominators, it is refreshing to know that Jaguar remains defiantly incomparable. For the name of the Jaguar dealer nearest you, call these numbers toll-free: (800) 447-4700, or, in Illinois, (800) 322-4400. British Leyland Motors Inc., Leonia, New Jersey 07605.

Jaguar XJ12, 1978

Peugeot 604. Europe is no longer keeping the best for itself.

The 604 is the best Peugeot made. And one of the best European touring sedans ever made. Every inch of the Peugeot 604 says luxury. And says even more about the person who owns one...without shouting.

Its design is timeless. Its craftsmanship is impeccable. And yet, for all its sensuous luxury, the Peugeot 604 is one of the most practical cars you can buy. It gives you the comfort of a living room. And the handling you'd expect of the most exquisitely engineered sports cars in the world.

Throughout Europe the 604 is often enjoyed as a chauffeur-driven touring sedan. But here you can enjoy an even greater privilege than the privileged class. The thrill of driving it yourself.

Peugeot 604. Europe is no longer keeping the best for itself. Now it's your turn.

For more information on buying, leasing, or overseas delivery see your Peugeot dealer. Or call 800-243-6000 toll free (in Connecticut call 1-800-882-6500). Peugeot Motors of America, Inc., Lyndhurst, New Jersey 07071.

PEUGEOT
No one builds cars the way we build cars.

Peugeot 604, 1978 ▶▶ *Oldsmobile Cutlass Salon, 1973*

Cutlass

Built in the Gran

The Grand Touring touches found in this sedan...

can now be found in this coupe.

Last year we created the Cutlass Salon sedan—Oldsmobile's version of a Grand Touring car. For '74, we've added a coupe.

Ever ridden in a real Grand Touring car? It makes you prefer winding side roads to busy freeways. Drive a Cutlass Salon and you'll see. There's a new, lower steering ratio for quicker response. Steel-belted radial tires. And front and rear anti-sway bars.

Now picture the inside of one of those expensive Grand Touring jobs. Contoured lounge seats, right? And they recline, right? So do Salon's. The upholstery is plush ribbed velour. And the console is the kind that makes you want to put nifty things in it.

There's also a Salon idea you won't find in those other cars. An Oldsmobile Rocket V8 teamed with Turbo Hydra-matic.

Oh, yes. Money. Salon doesn't have a Grand Touring price.

from Oldsmobile
Salon.
Touring tradition.

New Ford Ranchero...the pickup car!

If you've an idea Ford's all-new Ranchero is a high-spirited sports car, you're right. If you think Ranchero is a handy, hard-working pickup, right again. For Ranchero is a beautiful blending of both. It offers a ride that's both smoother and quieter with a wheelbase that's four inches longer than last year. New strength and durability with a solid big-car frame. And clean responsive handling with a new link coil rear suspension. Front disc brakes are standard, and you can choose any of six spirited engines up to a 429 V8. Big new loadspace, too, with a new box that's longer at the rail and wider at the floor. 4-foot panels easily slide between wheelhousings. And campers or boaters will welcome a new towing capacity of up to 6,000 pounds. See a Ranchero 500, GT or Squire at your Ford Dealer's soon. With so much that's so right, you can't go wrong.

A better idea for safety: Buckle up.

All-new FORD RANCHERO

Ford Ranchero, 1972

Economical Family Transportation Doesn't Have To Be Dull.
IT'S MORE FUN TO TAKE THE BUS.

Has the size of your family driven you into a car you can't afford? Does the car that fits your budget squeeze the fun out of your family? If so, you've missed the Bus. The 1978 Volkswagen Bus.

The '78 Bus costs less than most big station wagons. And to run, it's ahead by miles. The Bus' peppy, fuel-injected, two-liter engine is not only quiet, it's also very economical. It helps the Bus deliver an estimated 25 mpg on the highway, 17 in the city with standard transmission, according to the 1978 EPA tests. (Of course, actual mileage may vary depending on how and where you drive, optional equipment, such as automatic transmission, and the condition of your Bus.)

And nothing beats the Bus for family fun. It's easy to park, easy to handle, and it gives everyone in your family enough elbow room to relax in comfort. With space left over for your dog, your luggage, or just about anything else you want to carry. The Bus is 70% roomier inside than a full-sized domestic station wagon. And with the Bus' eight picture windows, everyone in the family gets the best seat in the house. And that's not all. The VW Bus is very versatile. The rear seat folds down to provide extra carrying space and that rear hatch and big sliding door lets you load everything from antiques to zithers.

So, when you want to uncramp your family's style, nothing compares to the Bus.

See your Volkswagen dealer today. And prove to yourself it's more fun to take the Bus. The 1978 Volkswagen Bus.

© Volkswagen of America, Inc.

Volkswagen Bus, 1978

Introducing the Jeep CJ/5 in "Jeans"

Look what the well dressed Jeep CJ/5 is wearing! New Levi's® styled seats with matching fold-down top. Made of rugged, easy to care for vinyl fabric in absolutely authentic styling—right down to the copper rivets. Built to take plenty of rough treatment and most anything the weather can dish out.

Choose Levi's® blue or Levi's® tan—to complement vehicle color.

The Levi's® interior is standard on the Jeep Renegade (shown above) and optional on the standard Jeep CJ/5.

Levi's® and Jeep Corporation—two names at home in the great outdoors—waiting for you! Jeep wrote the book on 4-wheel drive.

Jeep CJ/5

From a Subsidiary of
American Motors Corporation

Jeep CJ/5, 1974

Tough going? Go Bronco! From its heavy-duty front axle and exclusive Mono-Beam front suspension all the way back, the 4-wheel-drive Bronco is tough—durable—reliable. Maneuverability is outstanding. You can turn in a small 33.6-foot circle. High ground clearance lets you bull through high drifts. The same wide track front and rear provides excellent off-road stability. Bronco's a great family car, too, with well-appointed, comfortable interiors. Easy to handle or park. Doesn't ride like an ordinary 4-wheeler. 6 or V8 engines available (V8 required in California). Make a date with your wife—to see your Ford Dealer.

No roads at all? That's Bronco country.

Smooth highways–Bronco country, too.

tter idea for safety: Buckle up.

FORD BRONCO

Ford Bronco, 1972

New Ford Ranchero... Right on!

AM/FM Stereo Radio—with space-age microcircuitry, surrounds you in faithful stereo sound.

Hood Scoop Standard on GT Model— functional with Ram-Air induction on 351 (4V) and 429 V-8 engines.

Super Wide
G-70s—really grab the road when you want to hang in there.

High-back Bucket Seats—for individual comfort; high-back bench seat is standard.

Deluxe
Three-spoke Steering Wheel. Rim-blow feature gives fingertip horn control.

Performance Cluster—includes tachometer, odometer, clock, ammeter, water temperature and oil pressure gauges.

Four-on-the-floor—fully synchronized 4-speed transmission with quick-shift Hurst® mechanism.

Magnum 500
Chrome Wheels—the ultimate in "mag"-type wheels. Available on all models.

No question of who you are in a Ranchero, because your Ranchero can be a one-of-a-kind pickup, designed by you from a string of with-it options you wouldn't believe. Some are shown above. And

Ranchero's all new for '72. New size, new style, new engineering, new satisfaction. And the pickup box is both wider and longer. Visit your Ford Dealer and check the specs. Then roll your own!

A better idea for safety: Buckle up.

FORD RANCHERO

Ford Ranchero, 1972

All pickups are not created equal

Only Jeep Pickups offer Quadra-Trac™

Quadra-Trac is the new automatic 4-wheel drive system the experts are raving about. And only Jeep Pickups offer it. This new system delivers 4-wheel drive super-traction to the wheels the instant you need it. No need to get out and lock hubs, no shift lever to fuss with. Quadra-Trac is an exciting option that makes the toughest trucking smoother than ever before.

Whether you choose Quadra-Trac or our famous standard 4-wheel drive the

hauling's easier because both are the product of over 30 years of rough-road experience.

Add 'em up: The rugged dependability that Jeep has come to stand for—axles, suspension, body—all hanging together super-tough to do most any job you put it to, and Quadra-Trac, the premier 4-wheel drive. That adds up to one sweet pickup.

For fun or profit, Jeep Pickups are a little more equal than all the rest.

Jeep ◢◢ Truck

Jeep Pickups, 1974 ▶▶ *Chevrolet Chevelle, 1972*

Valley Trailer Center
The Best in the West

One of American Traveler's top dealerships is Valley Trailer Center in Sepulveda, California — they're among the best in the west! All of American Traveler's dealers share mutual pride in their products and your comfort and it makes them truly outstanding.

Stop in at Valley Trailer Center in Sepulveda. Visit their extensive parts store and twelve-bay service department, and see other top RV lines on display. You'll get a great offer — purchase an American Traveler at a competitive price, and get a great dealer free. He's not optional — he's standard.

VALLEY TRAILER CENTER
9005 SEPULVEDA BLVD.
SEPULVEDA, CA 91343, (213) 894-1106

A STAR IS BORN!

The '78 Omega by Chinook! The styling of the 80's today; designed and engineered to meet the demands of tomorrow. The sleek space-age styling features trouble-free fiberglass construction reinforced with a steel frame. Since the Omega is permanently mounted on a Toyota chassis, expect to get unbelievable gas mileage! (Approximately 20 MPG*)

The Omega offers such standard features as a commode; complete galley with sink, refrigerator and stove; loads of storage; sleeping space for four; sunroof; and full standup headroom. A complete motorhome!

Beneath the star-struck beauty of Omega is the Chinook reputation for quality and service integrity.

Test pilot the '78 Omega at Toyota dealers and RV centers today.

OMEGA

THE VERSATILE CONVERTIBLE WAGON.

Economy (25 MPG*), versatility, and aerodynamic styling all wrapped up in one. The Chinook MPG/Gazelle is perhaps the most unique vehicle available! It's a motorhome, station wagon and economy car all for about $7,995.

See it today at select Toyota dealers and RV centers across the country.

Join the Chinook experience! In a class by itself.

MPG/Gazelle

SU-28

CHINOOK

The leader in quality, economy motorhomes.
110 Newport Center Drive · Suite 250
Newport Beach, CA 92660

Please send more information!

☐ Omega ☐ Gazelle

NAME_____

ADDRESS_____

CITY_____STATE_____ZIP_____

Introducing Ranchero/77.

For the man in charge.

FORD

FORD DIVISION *Ford*

1977 Ford Ranchero—made for the man in charge.
    Outside, the Ranchero has been completely redesigned. Call it rakish, proud, daring, whatever. With its new GT-like appearance, vertically stacked headlamps, choice of 6 new exterior colors, and swooping shape . . . its new looks are bound to get looks.
    Inside, Ranchero lets you settle back into a world of performance options, new seat fabrics and optional leather-wrapped steering wheel or day/date analog clock. Most of all, Ranchero gives you the solid feeling of a well-built driving machine.
    The new redesigned Ford Ranchero. For the man who takes command of his life.

Built Ford Tough

93 out of 100 of all Ford Trucks registered over the last 12 years are still on the job.

Ford Ranchero/77, 1977

SCOUT® II BEATS BLAZER.
COMING AND GOING.

The 4-wheel drive Scout is trim where it counts, and more maneuverable than a Chevy Blazer. Scout's designed from the ground up to be a better performing off-road machine. It's 9½ inches narrower to get you through those tight spots Blazer can't handle. Five inches lower in overall height. But with the same ground clearance as Blazer.

Scout gives you a better approach angle than Blazer. Scout's 44% approach angle at its lowest point means you're far less likely to dig in and hang up your front end in those tough uphill conditions.

Scout is shorter with a tighter turning circle than Blazer. A full 3 feet 8 inches tighter. That's one heck of a difference when your turning around on a dead-end trail.

Scout carries more payload than Blazer. Scout's built tough to take it. And engineered to carry more. 35% more payload. That's an extra 643 pounds more than Blazer. Hundreds of pounds more gear, passengers, and camping equipment.

Scout has a longer cargo bed than Blazer. With rear seats up, Scout gives you nearly half a foot more cargo bed length than Blazer.

With Scout's rear seat folded forward and Blazer's stationary rear seat left bolted in place, Scout gives you 29 inches more usable cargo bed length than Blazer. For a total cargo bed length of almost 5 feet.

Scout conveniently gives you maximum cargo length by simply folding up the rear seat. But for maximum cargo length in a Blazer, you have to unbolt and leave your rear seat behind.

Find out for yourself what rugged design is all about. Test drive the incredible Scout II at your International Harvester dealer today.

Yes, I'm interested in more detailed information on Scout's design specs and off-road features. Please send me the brochures I've checked below. Enclosed is 50¢ for postage and handling. 706LBAM

☐ Scout*II
☐ Scout Traveler*
☐ Scout Terra™ Pickup
☐ Scout* Diesels
☐ Scout* Towing/RV Applications

Name _____
Please print
Phone _____
Address _____
City_____State____Zip____

Mail to: Scout Brochure
International Harvester
P.O. Box 1909, Mossville, Ill. 61552

SCOUT THE AMERICA OTHERS PASS BY.

IH INTERNATIONAL HARVESTER

The colors are red, white and blue.

The cars are Limited Edition Impalas, Novas and Vegas.

They're the special Spirit of America Chevrolets arriving at your Chevy dealer's right now.

They're cars known for their value. Distinctly styled with special interiors and equipment. Packaged like no Chevrolet before. Available for a limited time only.

Get the Spirit at your Chevy dealer's while they last.

The Spirit of America Impala package: • White or blue exterior. • Special white padded vinyl roof. • Special striping. • Special white wheels with paint stripes and trim rings. • Spirit of America crests. • Dual Sport mirrors, LH remote-control. • Wheel-opening moldings and fender skirts. • Bumper impact strips. • White all-vinyl interior trim with blue or red accents and carpeting. • Deluxe seat and shoulder belts. • Quiet Sound Group body insulation.

The Spirit of America Nova package: • White exterior. • Black touring-style vinyl roof. • Special striping. • Spirit of America decals. • White rally wheels with trim rings and special hubs. • Black dual Sport mirrors, LH remote-control. • Black grille. • E78-14 white-stripe tires. • White all-vinyl bucket seat interior. • Red carpeting.

The Spirit of America Vega package: • White exterior. • White vinyl roof. • Special striping. • Spirit of America decals. • White GT wheels with trim rings. • Custom Exterior. • Black-finished body sills. • White LH remote Sport mirror. • A70-13 white-lettered tires. • White all-vinyl Custom Interior. • Red carpeting.

Chevrolet

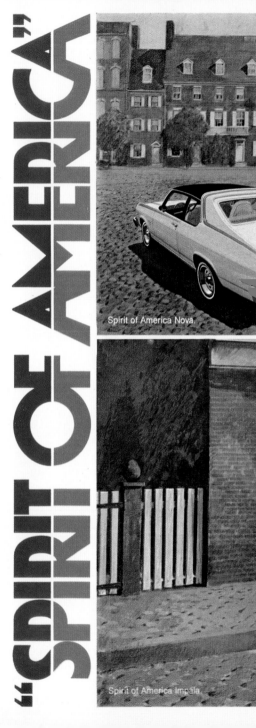

Spirit of America Nova.

Spirit of America Impala.

A limited edition of Chevrolets in Amerca's favorite colors.

Spirit of America Vega.

Dodge Aspen R/T.
For the person with driving ambition.

There are people who won't settle with just going along for the ride.

And it is to these people we dedicate the Dodge Aspen R/T.

Aspen R/T has a bold look. With a handsome blacked-out grille, wide rallye wheels, and distinctive stripes.

And its actions are quick. Decisive. Thanks to a proven 318 V8 engine and heavy-duty Isolated Transverse Suspension system.

Yet for all its remarkable attributes, Aspen R/T has a surprisingly low price.

As a matter of fact, *Motor Trend* magazine has found Dodge Aspen so unbelievable for its low price they named it
Car of the Year.

So if you have driving ambition, don't just go along for the ride. Drive the 1976 Dodge Aspen R/T

CHRYSLER

WE'RE LOOKING FOR PEOPLE WHO LOVE TO DRIVE.

We realize that, for some of you, driving an automobile is about as exhilarating as riding an escalator. That's sad.

Because with the right kind of car in your hands, the act of driving can be one of the truly pleasant things you do each day.

Which brings us to Camaro. In fact it brings lots of us to Camaro.

People who love to drive love Camaro because it's definitely a driver's car. It sits low and stands wide and moves like it really means it. Camaro is quick, quiet, tight and tough. All of which translates to a very special "feel". The spirit of Camaro. The lift the car can give you, even just driving to work.

If you love to drive, or would like to, take a turn in a '77 Camaro one day real soon.

Your Chevy dealer has one all gassed up and ready to go.

Driving gloves are optional.

Chevrolet

CAMARO

GM

MGB presents the world's biggest sunroof.

A super sunroof, a fully-convertible top that opens wide to let the sunshine in: it's standard equipment on every 1976 MGB. Along with the classic look and wide-open performance that have made MG famous for 50 years as one of the world's great sports car bargains.

MGB holds the Class E Championship in the Sports Car Club of America's national competition, as it has for four of the last five years.

Performances like this can't be faked: you can't fool a finish line with a flashy paint job or a fancy name. MGB's authentic sports car performance and crisp handling grow naturally out of standard equipment like radial tires, front disc brakes, short-throw, four-speed stick shift, rack and pinion steering and a race-proven 1798 cc engine.

If what you're driving makes you forget what fun is, take one MGB, fast. For the name of your nearest MGB dealer, call these toll-free numbers: (800) 447-4700, or, in Illinois, (800) 322-4400.

BRITISH LEYLAND MOTORS INC. LEONIA, NEW JERSEY 07605

MGB the wide-open sports car.

Pinto kicks up its heels for '77.

New style...sporty handling...proven performance.

FORD PINTO
FORD DIVISION *Ford*

977 Ford Pinto 3-door Runabout. Exciting new front and rear styling.

A high spirited California Pinto has been born for 1977. With a fresh new look that will still be exciting and distinctive years from now.

Pinto is spirited with new options, too. Like our new all-glass third door, a flip-up/removable open-air roof, Ford's new Variable Venturi carburation system, and a new 4-way driver's seat (it easily adjusts up and down, as well as fore and aft) for more convenience, more comfort.

One of our beautiful new interiors. Proof that the practical Pinto can also be luxurious.

Extras you don't pay extra for:

The '77 California Pinto is highly spirited with *extras that don't cost you extra.* Like steel-belted radial tires, deluxe

Steel-belted radials.

wheel covers, a special front stabilizer bar for sporty handling and an electric rear window defroster. All standard!

Rear window defroster.

But the beauty of the '77 Pinto doesn't stop with its new look and spirit. Critical areas

Front stabilizer bar.

around all front lights are now made of a new resilient material that's dent, chip and crack resistant under normal use ... and absolutely rustproof!

Deluxe wheel covers.

And to make sure your high spirited Pinto lasts, there's Pinto's built-in durability. Durability that starts with the electro-dip prime coating of Pinto's entire unit-body construction.

Find out how easy it is to corral the spirited '77 California Pinto. See your local Ford Dealer soon for a test drive.

Our most economically priced Ford Pinto, the Pinto Pony. Shown here with optional white sidewall tires.

**Ford's California Pinto.
The complete small car.**

STARFIRE.

MOVING THE BODY. AND THE MIND.

You're first attracted by the styling.
Sleek. Trim.
     You open the door and ease into the
high-backed bucket seats. You scan the
instrument panel as you take hold of the
padded sport steering wheel. Already your
mind is in motion.
     You push the available 5-speed stick
into gear. Starfire's available V-6 engine
responds.
          Sporty suspension and steel-belted
radials help make the going smooth. Front disc brakes are
there when you need them. You and the car become one.
The road is yours.
     Starfire SX. Transportation not only for your body.
But for your mind.

Oldsmobile
STARFIRE.
Can we build one for you?

GM

Oldsmobile Starfire SX, 1977

Datsun's new B-210 'Plus' gives you a
Nifty Fifty.

50 MPG HWY/37 MPG CITY.*

Plus all kinds of extras.
At Datsun, we don't think stripping a car down to boost gas mileage is the answer.
Which brings us to our new B-210 'Plus'. As you will see, we didn't strip it.
We stuffed it.
Plus 5-speed economy.
Among other things, it comes with a 5-speed.
Which works like overdrive. Thus, less fuel is used. And

there's less wear on the engine.
Plus extra value.
Now about those other things. Steel belted radial tires, sporty stripes, fully reclining bucket seats, carpeting, tinted glass, electric rear window defogger and power-assist front disc brakes are included in the B-210 'Plus'.
So you see, while this car gets lots of miles per gallon, you get lots of car.
Plus tough.
From start to acrylic paint

finish, it's tough all over.
For example, its solid unibody is all steel from hood to hatch.
In short, Datsun's new B-210 'Plus' has lots of strong pluses going for it.

*(1977 EPA estimates. Your actual mileage may differ, depending on how and where you drive, the condition of your car and its optional equipment. California mileage figures slightly lower.)

Suddenly it's going to dawn on you.
DATSUN SAVES

Datsun B-210, 1977   ▶▶ *Ford Thunderbird, 1977*

THUNDERBIRD

FORD DIVISION *Ford*

Raise the roof tonight in a Dodge Charger.

If you can't wait to see that evening sun go down, the '77 Charger is your special car. Made for people who come out to play after dark. And now you can make a night of it in a Charger that welcomes the night inside.

Just remove the transparent panels of the optional T-bar roof, and you're cruising in a Charger that's almost a convertible. Come alive in the invigorating breeze as you settle into the high-back bucket seats. For certain, you and your Charger were born for the night.

A standard 318 V8 teams up with TorqueFlite automatic transmission to give Charger a response that's anything but everyday.

When the day starts to fade and you're ready to shift into high gear, you need the car that can light up the night—Charger. Why let another sun go down without driving one? You can buy or lease an exciting new '77 Charger from your nearby Dodge Dealer today.

Dodge

THE NIGHT BELONGS TO CHARGER.

A PRODUCT OF CHRYSLER CORPORATION

Dodge Charger, 1977

The new Volaré T-Bar Roof: our answer to the vanishing convertible.

To the new generation of Americans who have never known the driving pleasure of wind through the hair, we proudly dedicate our new T-Bar Volaré Coupe.

It feels just as good as it looks.

It feels free and fresh when open.

Sound and secure when closed.

But be advised; when you close it, you're in no way closed in. Because the dual pop-in roof panels are made of a thick, rich smoked glass. So you can easily look up and out at the world. While the world has a hard time looking in.

The optional T-Bar roof joins a big list of Volaré

standard comforts that includes big, wide windows; big, wide seats; and, of course, the remarkable isolated transverse suspension.

As novel as the name implies, the isolated transverse suspension system imparts a smooth quality to Volaré's ride . . . a ride like that of bigger cars.

C'mon, slip into something more comfortable: the new Volaré T-Bar, it's the original topless feeling.

A matchless feeling you can buy or lease as near as your nearest Chrysler-Plymouth Dealer.

Plymouth

A PRODUCT OF CHRYSLER CORPORATION

Plymouth Volaré. The small car with the accent on comfort.

Plymouth Volaré T-Bar, 1977

Introducing the Lincoln Versailles.

Engineering made it happen.
Now, a car with a 110-inch wheelbase, with a superb luxury car ride.

Now there is a new luxury car similar in size to the finest European luxury cars, with the smooth, quiet, distinctly luxurious ride of an American luxury car. It is the new Lincoln Versailles and, like the bridging of a river, the construction of a tower, its ride is a true engineering achievement.

Lincoln Versailles is engineered for smoothness; its major components are balanced to critical tolerances.

An investment in engineering.

Lincoln Versailles is engineered for quietness and insulated to reduce external noise.

Lincoln Versailles is engineered for luxury and fully equipped with standard features as significant as four-wheel disc brakes and as luxurious as a unique 'Clearcoat' paint finish.

Test-drive Lincoln Versailles. You will quickly understand its uniqueness, and the many benefits of its engineering, in the Lincoln Continental tradition.

LINCOLN VERSAILLES

LINCOLN-MERCURY DIVISION

Lincoln Versailles, 1977

▶ *Pontiac Phoenix, 1977*

PHOENIX by PONTIAC

This is the first Pontiac Phoenix. It's our new six-passenger luxury compact. And it typifies the special way we feel about cars.

We think a car's styling should be clean. Strong. Arresting. Like our new Phoenix.

We think a car should be comfortable, but not overbearing. So we gave Phoenix full-width seats with a fold-down center armrest. Really nice fabrics. Cut-pile carpet. Padded door panels. A very functional

instrument panel. Even a cushioned steering wheel. They give Phoenix a quiet kind of luxury we think you'll like.

We think a car should move down the road with authority. With its standard V-6 or available V-8, Phoenix does.

We think Phoenix is a pretty special compact. The kind you've been waiting to buy or lease. That's why it's arriving at your Pontiac dealer's now.

 PONTIAC THE MARK OF GREAT CARS

1978 Buick Regal

Is it possible? Romance and realism —in one car? How can such things be?

Well, we can assure you that building such a car is no small feat. But it can be done. And we built the new

attention to matters of efficiency and function.

Consider, for example, the fact that the new Regal is much trimmer than last year's model. To make it more

down-to-earth qualities? All right. How about the fact that it gives you more trunk room, more head room and more leg room than last year's coupe? How about the new 3.2 litre (196-cu.-in.) even-firing V-6 that comes as standard equipment? It got, according to the EPA, an estimated 33 mpg in the highway test, 19 in the city, and 23 mpg combined when equipped with a manual transmission (powertrain not available in California). Or an available 231-cu.-in. (3.8 litre) V-6 with automatic transmission that got an estimated 27 mpg in the highway test, 19 in the city and 22 combined. (This V-6 powertrain

It doesn't take up a lot of room outside.

mid-size Buick Regal to prove it.

Outwardly, the shape is clean. Uncluttered. Downright impossible not to marvel at. And on the inside, it's pure magic. In the way it looks. The way it feels. And the effect it has on the psyche. All in all, as we said, a dream car.

Yet, in this same dashing package, you'll also find an equal measure of

But it gives you a lot of room inside.

maneuverable in city traffic. Easier to park. Want more evidence of Regal's

Turbocharging: The power you want from the six cylinders you need. Will wonders never cease?

Down-to-earth dream car.

quired in California and EPA
nates are lower there.) Your mileage
vary depending on how and where
drive, the car's condition, and how
quipped.
Regal Coupe and Limited models

**y people love going
ces in
uick.**

are equipped with GM-built engines
supplied by various divisions. See your
Buick dealer for details.

Anyway, you get
the point. Regal is a
pretty amazing com-
bination of the things
you want and the things
you need in a car. And
we suppose we could stop
here.

But there's one more little bit
of Buick science and magic that really
makes our case. It's the Regal Sport
Coupe. It's powered by a
3.8 litre (231-cu.-in.)
turbocharged V-6 engine.

Turbocharged by exhaust gases,
it offers the passing power you want

It tells you everything.

from the six cylinders you need.
Incredible.

The new Regal.
What it is, is a little science.
And a little magic.
At your Buick dealer.

BUICK
A little science. A little magic.

The new AMC Concord D/L.
Now you don't have to pay extra for the luxury of a luxury compact.

The Concord D/L is a new luxury compact that comes with all its luxury intact. Not tacked on as extras for an extra few hundred dollars.

For no extra charge you get: a landau roof with opera windows. Color-keyed wheel covers and whitewalls. Crushed velour individual reclining seats. A wood-grained dash with a digital clock. And lots of other luxury features that you'd expect to be charged extra for.

Perhaps the nicest luxury of all is the smooth, quiet ride that AMC has engineered into the Concord D/L, with a new suspension system and insulation network against road shock and sound.

You also get AMC's exclusive BUYER PROTECTION PLAN,® with the only full 12 month /12,000 mile warranty. That means AMC will fix, or replace free any part, except tires, for 12 months or 12,000 miles whether the part is defective, or just plain wears out under normal use and service. AMC also has a plan to provide a free loaner car should guaranteed repairs take overnight.

So if you've been thinking about a Volare, or Granada, or another luxury compact, think about this: the new Concord D/L is the luxury compact with no extra charge for the luxury.

AMC ◢◣ Concord D/L
The luxury Americans want. The size America needs.

Available in 2-door, 4-door and wagon models.

AMC Concord D/L, 1977

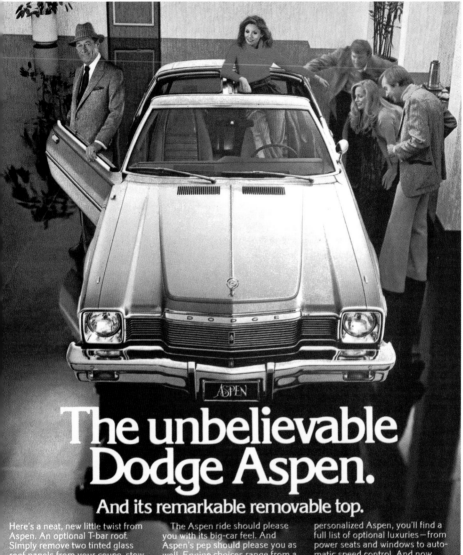

The unbelievable Dodge Aspen.

And its remarkable removable top.

Here's a neat, new little twist from Aspen. An optional T-bar roof. Simply remove two tinted glass roof panels from your coupe, stow them in your trunk...and you've got the feel of a convertible. Unbelievable, that's the Aspen way. All the style you insist on in a coupe, with a size that's very practical.

The Aspen ride should please you with its big-car feel. And Aspen's pep should please you as well. Engine choices range from a standard 225 one-barrel Six to an optional 360 four-barrel V8, and include the popular new Dodge Super Six. Check your Dealer for availability details.

And should you want a more personalized Aspen, you'll find a full list of optional luxuries—from power seats and windows to automatic speed control. And now there's even a T-bar roof. Another great accessory you can add to the Aspen you buy or lease.

The small car at a small price...the unbelievable

Dodge Aspen, 1977

NEW CHEVY MONZA.

FEWER YEN, MARKS, LIRA, FRANCS, OR BUCKS THAN ANY SPORTY FOREIGN HATCHBACK.

'78 Chevy Monza 2+2 Hatchback Coupe.

As a matter of fact, this new Chevy Monza is priced lower than all imported hatchbacks, except Honda Civic, Mazda GLC, Plymouth Arrow, and Renault LeCar. That slick little fastback hatchback shown above, equipped with available sport mirrors and wheel moldings, is priced $1,678* less than a Toyota Celica GT Liftback. And $2,034* less than a VW Scirocco.

$3661.*

Chevrolet

*Price and price comparisons based on manufacturers' suggested retail prices including dealer preparation. Tax, license, destination charges, and available equipment extra. Prices differ in California.

So if you're looking for a sporty car, compare Chevy Monza to the foreign sports. It's quite a car at quite a price. No matter what language you speak.

SEE WHAT'S NEW TODAY IN A CHEVROLET.

Chevrolet Monza, 1978

The AMC Gremlin.
More fun than a barrel of gas bills.

The Gremlin is an economical small car with the room, ride and comfort of a bigger car. It's economical because it has an efficient 4-cylinder engine and 4-speed gear box, which manage to be very thrifty and very peppy at the same time.

The Gremlin also comes with a lot of things that make it more fun to drive. 4 on the floor, wide-track handling and easy maneuverability, give the Gremlin quite a sporty feel. And casual Levi seats, racing stripes and slot style wheels give the Gremlin X quite a sporty look to go with it.

You also get AMC's exclusive BUYER PROTECTION PLAN, with the only full 12 month/12,000 mile warranty. That means AMC will fix, or replace free any part, except tires, for 12 months or 12,000 miles whether the part is defective, or just plain wears out under normal use and service.

Discover how much fun, and how economical, driving can be with a perky, practical Gremlin.

Based on EPA estimated ratings, 35 highway, 22 city, 27 combined for the optional 4-cylinder engine with 4-speed manual transmission. Your actual mileage may vary depending on your car's condition, optional equipment, and how and where you drive. California figures lower.

AMC■ Gremlin
The fun Americans want. The size America needs.

® BUYER PROTECTION PLAN is reg. U.S. Pat. and Tm. Off.

AMC Gremlin, 1977

Our lowest priced Honda isn't so simple.

The Honda Civic®1200 Sedan is our lowest priced Honda.* We hope that statement doesn't put you off.

We know that lots of people tend to be suspicious when they see the words "lowest priced." Especially when it's a car. They immediately think of some stripped-down model calculated to snag the unwary buyer by means of a seductive price tag.

That's why we're running this ad. To let you know that, despite its very reasonable price, the Civic 1200 Sedan gives you such traditional Honda engineering refinements as transverse-mounted engine, front-wheel drive, rack and pinion steering, power-assisted dual-diagonal braking system with front discs, and four-wheel independent MacPherson strut suspension.

And that's not all. The Civic 1200 Sedan abounds with standard features that other manufacturers might charge you extra for.

*Not available in Calif. and high altitude areas. Manufacturer's suggested retail price excluding freight, tax, license, title, and options.
©1978 American Honda Motor Co., Inc. Civic 1200 is a Honda trademark.

Honda Civic 1200 Sedan, 1978

These include reclining bucket seats, adjustable head rests, wall-to-wall carpeting, opening rear-quarter windows, inside hood release, rear-seat ash tray, plus the instrument cluster shown opposite, a simple layout that nonetheless provides the added convenience of a trip odometer.

Like our other two Honda cars – the Civic CVCC® and the Honda Accord® – the Civic 1200 doesn't need a catalytic converter and runs on unleaded or money-saving regular gasoline.

So there you have it. The Honda Civic 1200 Sedan. Because it's a Honda, it's a simple car. But not so simple as its price would lead you to believe.

HONDA
We make it simple.

"I take a break from life's little problems, behind the wheel of my Mustang."

Go Mustang

FORD — When America needs a better idea, Ford puts it on wheels.

Lose yourself in the sporty spirit of the '78 Ford Mustang II. Let this elegant Ghia take you away from an ordinary day. Or maybe you'd like the wide-open T-Roof Convertible, or the 3-door Hatchback. And you can opt for a Rallye Package, oversize tires, choose from 5 different kinds of wheels, 7 different interiors, and 14 great exterior colors. So visit your Ford Dealer and go Mustang. It could make your life a lot more fun.

FORD MUSTANG II
FORD DIVISION

75th ANNIVERSARY

Ford Mustang II, 1977

▶ *Datsun 200-SX, 1977*

200-SX

Suddenly from Datsun:
A sporty car with everything
but a sports car price.

Exit dull, sluggish economy cars. Enter Datsun's spicy 200-SX. Sweet-handling. Tasty appointments. And no bitter price to swallow.

Enjoy.

Fun and frugal 5-speed.

Sporty 5-speed transmission works like overdrive. So it not only zips around traffic, it saves wear and tear on the engine. About the engine: it's the 2-liter single overhead cam type. The type sports cars are made of. All of which makes the 200-SX anything but dull.

Extras, yes. Extra cost, no.
· AM/FM multiplex stereo radio
· Steel belted radial tires
· Tachometer
· Fully reclining bucket seats
· Cut-pile carpeting
· Electric rear window defogger
· Tinted glass
· Electric clock
· Sporty 5-speed gearbox
· Power-assist front disc brakes

All for under $4500. (Manufacturer's Suggested Retail Price not including destination charges, taxes, license or title fees and optional tape stripe and mag-type wheel cover package.)

Tough sport.

Solid, all-steel unibody is but one example of how the Datsun 200-SX is put together to stay together. Fact is, when we made this fun little car, we made sure of one thing.

The fun would last.

Suddenly it's going to dawn on you.

DATSUN SAVES

48 HIGHWAY, 36 CITY.
IT RUNS ON QUALITY.

DATSUN B-210 GX. It took Datsun dedication to create this champ. With its optional five-speed stick, B-210 GX is rated the No. 1 highway gas mileage car. An astonishing 48 highway, 36 city.

And built to endure—with an engine that has won five straight SCCA racing championships; with an aluminum cylinder head to reduce weight; with a front end that never needs alignment for caster or camber in normal use; with devotion to detail— even painting the _inside_ of the air cleaner. If you think that sounds zealous—you're right. That's exactly what we mean when we say "We Are Driven."

And every mile is comfortable, solid, sporty...because of B-210 GX standards: steel-belted radials, power front disc brakes, fully reclining front bucket seats, tinted glass—and a lot more. Want more? Automatic transmission and factory air conditioning are available options. It took Datsun ingenuity to conceive it—and Datsun determination to achieve it. B-210 GX. Quality like this is no accident.

48 MPG HWY.	36 MPG CITY.

EPA estimate. Your actual mileage may differ, depending on how and where you drive, the condition of your car and its optional equipment. California mileage lower.

Sporty 5-speed stick

Fade-resistant power front disc brakes

NOBODY DEMANDS MORE FROM A DATSUN THAN DATSUN.

DATSUN
WE ARE DRIVEN

THE NAME OF QUALITY
NISSAN
NISSAN MOTORS

Miles & Miles of Heart

me&my ARROW

Datsun B-210 GX, 1978 ◄

Plymouth Arrow, 1977

1979 Oldsmobile Ninety-Eight Regency. Of the world's luxury automobiles, it could be the most logical choice.

One look tells you the 98 Regency is an impressive luxury car.
Within its solid Body by Fisher, richness and comfort abound. But in a changing
world, a luxury car must have its practical side as well. And that's the beautiful logic
of a 98 Regency. Advanced engineering has created a big, roomy car with comfort for
six and a smooth, luxury ride—yet it's surprisingly maneuverable in crowded city traffic.
Its response to your command is impressively easy and quick. And you get the added luxury
of impressive fuel economy, as well. With the standard 5.7-litre (350 CID) V8, EPA estimates
are 21 mpg highway, 15 city; with the available 5.7-litre diesel V8, they're 29 mpg highway,
21 city!* Still another impressive aspect is the 98 Regency price. Compare it to those of other
cars of its size and luxury. You may be pleasantly surprised. And, many Olds dealers offer
the option to buy or lease your Regency. No wonder 98 Regency is considered the
thinking man's luxury car. Test-drive one soon, and discover just how logical a
luxury car can be. *Your mileage may vary depending on how you drive,
your car's condition and equipment. Gasoline mileage lower in Calif.

Oldsmobile 98 Regency, 1979

Oldsmobile

98 Regency

Have one built for you.

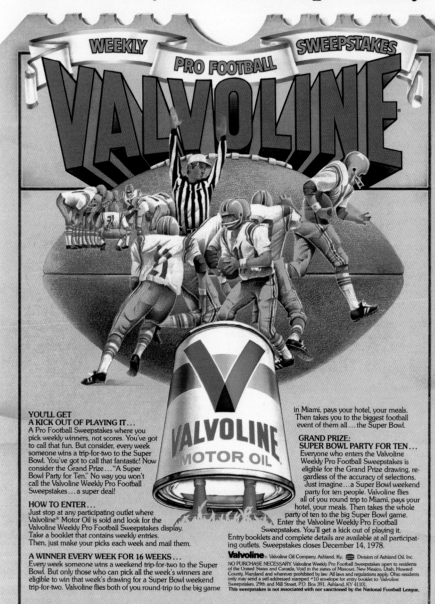

Valvoline Motor Oil, 1978 ▶ *Cragar Custom Wheels, 1978* ▶▶ *Ford Cruising Wagon and Van, 1*

ON THE STREET.

Bright chrome is in. So is Cragar with a trio that really shines. The popular spoked S/S has always been the custom wheel king. Now, it has a pair of regal companions in the solid SS/T and Slick Dish with Wire Basket. A royal selection of applications and sizes in all three. Cragar does it – on the street.

Ford. First in vans by a comfortable margin.

Shown with owner-added striping. Wheels shown are optional. Check your local Ford Dealer for availability.

Customized for "Cruising."

Industry's first customized van. Factory built fully—inside and out—a look that sets you apart in a crowd.

Loads of livin' room

Add your great ideas to ours. Optional swivel Captain's Chairs, too!

Ford's out front in vans—in more ways than one. First with the van concept about 15 years ago. And first with an advanced out-front design. We moved the engine forward so you have more room and downright comfort. And did a lot more. Put yourself in the leader in vans—put yourself in a Ford!

Wild! Ford's new "Cruising" Wagon.

Part wagon, part van, all fun. Ford's restyled Pinto wagon up front, wide open van room in rear. An Industry exclusive!

Ford Vans—fun to get into.

It's the easiest van to get in, out and move around in that Ford ever built!

93 out of 100 of all Ford Trucks registered over the last 12 years are still on the job.

FORD

FORD DIVISION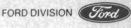

Every so often, a few lucky people get the chance to buy a great new sports car.

Now it's your turn.
Mazda RX-7.

A car like this doesn't come along very often. If you ever wished you had been there to shake up the car world with the new MG-TC back in 1947, with a 1953 Corvette when it was heresy on wheels, a 240-Z in 1970 when it turned more heads than hot pants...then you understand.

The 1979 RX-7 is the kind of car that makes your stomach muscles tighten when you start it. That lures you through a corner with a flick of the wrist and a rap of exhaust. It's the real thing: a sports car with all the traditional virtues and then some.

One of those traditional virtues is performance. Acceleration from 0 to 50 mph in 6.3 seconds. Cornering that comes from its refined suspension, the bite of its fat, steel-belted radial tires. Braking from a power-assisted combination of ventilated discs in front, finned drums in back.

But there are some highly untraditional virtues, too. The RX-7 was designed specifically to take advantage of the Mazda rotary engine's unique combination of compactness,

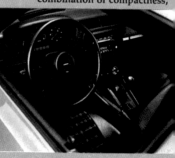

Mazda RX-7, 1978

1947.
The MG-TC.

1953.
The Corvette.

1970.
The 240-Z.

smoothness and high performance. It made some important differences.

The compactness made possible a front mid-engine design, providing nearly perfect weight distribution for impeccable handling and smooth ride. It also made possible the RX-7's slick, wind-cheating lines.

At the same time, the smooth power and broad, flat torque curve of the Mazda rotary make the RX-7 a real stormer, but one that's easy to get along with at low speeds.

If you thought you'd never own one of the great sports cars, better test drive a Mazda RX-7

GS-Model (shown) or S-Model. You simply have to experience it from the driver's seat to understand what this car is all about: the kind of comfort, versatility and room you've always wanted, the kind of performance you've always dreamed of. And all at a price you'll find hard to believe.

Believe. Your time has come. The Mazda RX-7 is here.

*POE price for S-Model: $6,395. For GS-Model shown: $6,995. (Slightly higher in California.) Taxes, license, freight and optional equipment are extra. (Wide alloy wheels shown above $250 extra.) Mazda's rotary engine licensed by NSU-WANKEL

From $6,395*

GS-Model shown: $6,995.*

The car you've been waiting for is waiting for you.

Consumer Orientation
No. 3 in a Series
Subject: Introduction
of the Porsche 924 Turbo

Porsche 924 Turbo

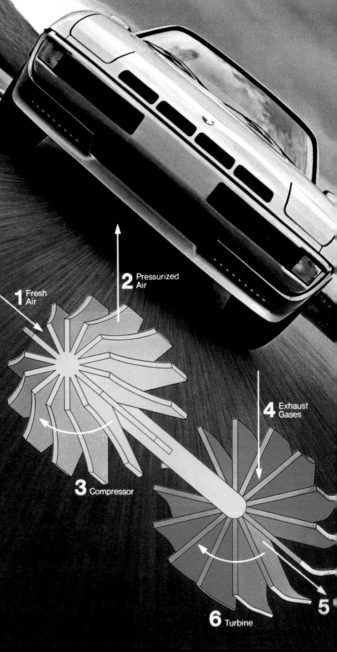

The Porsche 924 Turbo. On the track at Weissach, it covers the quarter mile from a standing start in 16.3 seconds. Its speed at the ¼-mile mark is 88 mph. Its maximum speed: 132 mph. The 924 Turbo is a direct descendant of the 917 Can-Am champion, the Porsche that made turbocharging practical for road racers. Prior to the 917, turbo-charged automobiles suffered from poor throttle response and reliability. But the 917 Turbo solved these problems with its unique bypass valve and wastegate control system—standard equipment on the new 924 Turbo.

1. The KKK turbocharger draws in fresh air.
2. The compressor forces the air/fuel mixture into the engine cylinders under pressure. Because the turbocharged engine receives more air/fuel than a naturally-aspirated engine, its combustion is greater. And its horsepower is increased without increasing its engine displacement. Thus, while the 924 Turbo's engine displaces only 1984 cc, it develops 143 hp at 5500 rpm.
3. The 924 Turbo has almost instantaneous throttle response because of its bypass valve. When the throttle is closed, the valve opens and routes the pressurized air harm-lessly back through the compressor in a closed loop. This maintains turbine speed. So when boost is demanded, the turbine does not have to be re-accelerated. Boost is available again in only 0.1 second.
4. Hot, normally-wasted, engine exhaust gases drive the turbine which is connected by a common shaft to the compressor.
5. The gases vent by way of the exhaust line and muffler. A waste-gate is located upstream of the turbine to control the excess gases not required to power the turbine.

At Porsche, we design a car as a total system. And so the 924 Turbo has a new cylinder head. A stronger driveshaft. New spoilers: front and rear. In fact, it has the lowest drag coefficient of any street Porsche: 0.35. And as a result of its total design efficiency, it requires only 16.5 horsepower to cruise at 55 mph.

For more information on the 924 Turbo, call toll free: (800) 447-4700. In Illinois, (800) 322-4400.

1 Fresh Air

2 Pressurized Air

3 Compressor

4 Exhaust Gases

5

6 Turbine

LEASE A LEGEND. THE PORSCHE 924.

Why lease an ordinary car when you can lease a new 1979 Porsche?

The Porsche 924.

It's designed to carry on the Porsche tradition of winning. A tradition that spans 31 years and includes over 400 major racing victories.

It's also designed for the practicality of today. Its unique rear transaxle provides virtually perfect 50-50 weight distribution between front and rear—for balanced road holding and braking.

Its aerodynamic design is aesthetically pleasing—and practical. In wind tunnel tests, it registers an amazingly low drag co-efficient of only 0.36.

Best of all, even with options, leasing a 924 is surprisingly affordable.

So visit your Porsche + Audi dealer and test drive a living legend.

PORSCHE + AUDI
NOTHING EVEN COMES CLOSE

Porsche 924 Turbo, 1979 ◄

Porsche 924, 1979

GOOD NEWS FOR PEOPLE 7'2" AND UNDER.

If you've always thought a little car meant a lot of crowding, you've obviously never looked into a Volkswagen Rabbit.

There happens to be so much room in a Rabbit that all 7'2" of Wilt Chamberlain can fit comfortably into the driver's seat.

With space left over.

Because the Rabbit has even more headroom than a Rolls-Royce.

As well as more room for people and things than practically every other imported car in its class.

Including every Datsun. Every Toyota. Every Honda, Mazda, and Renault.

Not to mention every small Ford and Chevy.

And, of course, what's all the more impressive about the room you get in a Rabbit is that it comes surrounded by the Rabbit itself. The car that, according to Car and Driver Magazine, "...does more useful and rewarding things than any other small car in the world..."

So how can you go wrong?

With the Rabbit you not only get the comfort of driving the most copied car in America.

You also get the comfort of driving a very comfortable car.

Because it may look like a Rabbit on the outside.

But it's a Rabbit on the inside.

VOLKSWAGEN DOES IT AGAIN

Nothing performs like a Saab.

turbo

The new Saab 900 Turbo 5-door. Its combination of performance, appointments, and sedan convenience are rare in today's world of sameness.

The performance car perfected.

At its heart is the Saab turbo engine. Saab engineers took the kind of power that dominates the big race tracks like Indianapolis and LeMans and harnessed it to work at everyday driving speeds. They did this by designing a turbocharging system that puts out more torque at lower engine speeds. So when you have to pass, or merge into fast moving traffic, there's an incredible surge of power at your disposal.

A feel for the road.

In addition to having extraordinary power, the new Saab Turbo is uniquely equipped to control it. A longer wheelbase, new suspension geometry and front wheel drive give the car cat-like agility – even on rain, snow and ice. Bilstein gas shocks and rack and pinion steering help you

cling to the road. Power-assisted 4-wheel disc brakes help the Michelin TRX radial tires come to smooth, sure stops.

Sports car excitement/Sedan comfort

The new Turbo 5-door will carry a family of five in style and comfort. The interior is of soft velour. Front seats are fully reclining and heated. Air conditioning, power steering, and a sliding sunroof made of steel are standard.

Engineered in Sweden, this is truly a car in a class by itself. For convenience, excitement, and sheer driving pleasure, nothing performs like a Saab Turbo 5-door.

SAAB 900

Standard du
assisted spo

Concealed adjustable headrests.

Standard

Standard inside deck re

Standard adjustable
lumbar supports

Plymouth Sapporo, 1978

Standard tachometer, oil and amp gauges and trip odometer.

el.

Standard tilt steering column.

Standard forced air ventilation.

Optional air conditioning.

Optional AM-FM radi with cassette.

Standard 5-speed transmission (Automatic shown, optional).

Optional power windows.

Standard memory-lock seats for ease of rear entry.

THE '78 FORD BRONCO.

COMPARE IT TO ANY 4-WHEELER, ANYWHERE.

The first 4-wheeler that puts it all together.
Introducing Ford's all-new Bronco with... 1. Big cube 5.8L (351) V-8 standard... 2. Choice of part-time 4 WD with optional automatic... 3. Rear foot-well for seating comfort... 4. Rear flip-fold seat option for usable cargo space... 5. Four-speed transmission... 6. Front quad shock option... 7. Free Wheeling package option... 8. Off-road handling package option... 9. Privacy™ Glass option... 10. Choice of bucket or optional front bench seats... 11. Front stabilizer bar. Bronco: Winner of the Four Wheeler Of The Year award from Four Wheeler magazine, October 1977.

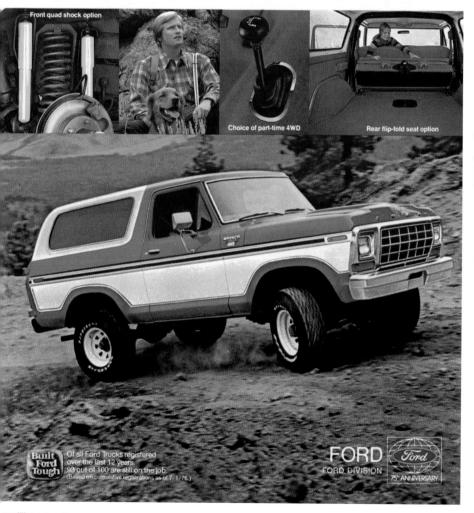

Front quad shock option

Choice of part-time 4WD

Rear flip-fold seat option

Built Ford Tough Of all Ford Trucks registered over the last 12 years, 93 out of 100 are still on the job. (Based on cumulative registrations as of 7/1/76.)

FORD — FORD DIVISION — Ford 75th ANNIVERSARY

Free-Wheelin' Fords. They're TNT!

Free Wheeling means factory-customized trucks with dazzling interiors, special paints, trick wheels and blacked-out grilles. Start with the Free Wheeling Styleside pickup shown below with rainbow stripes, blacked-out grille and front bumper, forged aluminum wheels (4), RWL sport tires. New Free Wheeling Fords. They're TNT. And they're ready at your Ford Dealer.

● **Free Wheeling Bronco**
Comes equipped with black bumpers, mirrors, sport steering wheel, swooping tricolor tape treatment, spoke wheels and RWL tires.

● **Free Wheeling Courier**
Get it with wide oval RWL tires, cast styled aluminum wheels (4), GT bar, push bar, fog lamps, custom accent tape stripes, and more.

● **Free Wheeling Van**
Includes sport steering wheel, black painted rocker panels, black front/rear bumpers and mirrors. A separate interior package option is also available. Van shown with additional factory options, owner-added stripes.

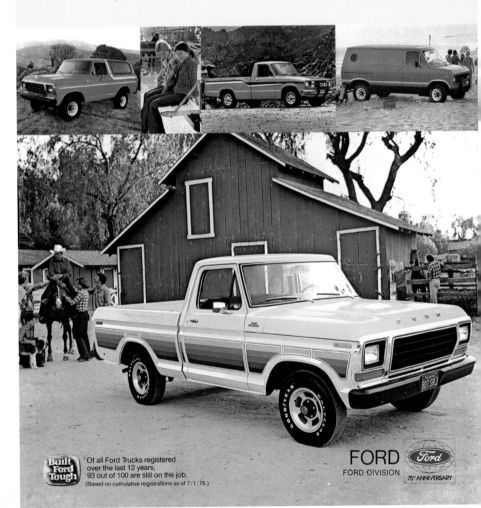

Built Ford Tough

'Of all Ford Trucks registered over the last 12 years, 93 out of 100 are still on the job. (Based on cumulative registrations as of 7/1/76.)

FORD *Ford*
FORD DIVISION
75ᵀᴴ ANNIVERSARY

Jeep Wagoneer *Limited*

The ultimate wagon

Some bikes challenge egos.

You don't just jump on a Bonnie and take off.
The Bonneville is a motorcycle that demands involvement.
A vertical twin that insists you learn exactly how to tickle the carbs...
throttle just right...
so one healthy kick brings it roaring to life.
Bonneville riders—over two generations of them—understand and appreciate
this intimate bond between man and machine.
Most egos aren't up to the kind of a trip that today's 750cc Bonnie demands.
But if yours is, we have a most rewarding motorcycle for you.

1261 State College Parkway, Anaheim, California 92806 **The Bonneville for '77.** NVT AMERICA
CIRCLE NO. 22 ON READER SERVICE PAGE.

showroom showdown

$1998.

CB-750K The brand-new 1977 CB-750K is a great machine. The eighth-generation son of the first of the modern-day superbikes. An overhead-cam, four-cylinder, four-stroke engine powers this stylish, proven performer. And now it's being listed at the manufacturer's suggested retail price of only $1,998.* That's right, $1,998. Hundreds of dollars less than you might expect. And that $1,998 price is not a specially-reduced sale price. That's the everyday price which this year includes all set-up charges.

This year the 750K has received some really neat performance and comfort changes. Like carburetors equipped with an accelerator pump for snappier throttle response, a new five-gallon tank, four seamless mufflers, recontoured seat and new handlebars with soft neoprene grips. There are exposed-leg, free-valve-type hydraulic front forks, a new 17-inch rear rim and 4.50 cross-section tire for better ride. Plus the one feature that comes standard on every Honda motorcycle—proven Honda reliability. At only $1,998 it's a great way to go. The new 1977 CB-750K has never been better, nor has the time to buy one.

going strong in the showroom!

HONDA

THERE IS NO BIGGER STREET

The Harley-Davidson Super Glide.

IKE.

PONTIAC GRAND AM

When we created the fabled Grand Am in '73, we attracted quite a following. A spirited bunch who loved the way it cornered. And climbed. And smoothed out little wrinkles in the road.

This year, that loyal group has reason to be elated. Because we've brought Grand Am back. In all its glory.

This time around, it's trimmer. Yet surprisingly roomy. And with all the good stuff that makes Grand Am a Grand Am.

It challenges roads with a feisty 301 cubic-inch 2-bbl. V-8.* And an automatic transmission. Both standard.

It takes on curves with a passion. Thanks to Rally Radial Tuned Suspension. Steel-belted radials. Power steering and power brakes.

It indulges the driver with deep notchback seats. Deluxe cushion soft-rim steering wheel. And distinctive recessed dash offering easy access to everything.

It dazzles passersby with virile good looks. A vertical ported grille. And bold new two-tone paint treatment.

Experience the new Grand Am for yourself. Drive it. Bask in it. And before you know it, you'll be a loyal follower, too.   1978 ▼ Pontiac's best year yet!

*305 CID 2-bbl. V-8 in California. Engines produced by various GM divisions. See your dealer.

WE BROUGHT IT BACK ALIVE.

Let the Spirit move you

Available in sedan or liftback.
® Buyer Protection Plan is reg. US Pat. and TM Off.

There's a new excitement in small cars. The brand-new 1979 Spirit DL from American Motors. This car's got more than corduroy bucket seats, a sleek instrument panel, sporty looks and a great ride. It's got more than the exclusive AMC Buyer Protection Plan.®

This car's got spirit.
The new 1979 Spirit, from AMC.

AMC ◢ SPIRIT

Ford introduces FUTURA

A combination of styling and technology for 1978...and beyond

Here is a car for the automotive future. With dynamic styling inside and out. Comfort for five passengers, yet fuel and cost efficiency for the years ahead. A car realistically priced for today. The new Futura. Before you consider any other car available today, read on...

Scheduled Maintenance 50,000 miles about $150.*

Futura is a car engineered to hold down the costs of maintenance. Ford estimates that with automatic transmission and Futura's standard engine,

nance will cost only about $150. (*Based on Ford labor time standards, a $14.50/hour labor rate and Ford's suggested parts prices in effect Aug., 1977.)

33 MPG (hwy) 23 MPG (city)

Futura's EPA mileage estimates—with 2.3 litre engine and manual 4-speed— are the highest of any car in its class. Of course, your actual mileage may vary depending on how you drive, your car's condition and optional equipment. Calif. ratings are lower. Futura is also available with 3.3 litre 6-cylinder and

$4,267 as shown

Futura's sticker price excluding taxes, title and destination charges.

Visit your local Ford Dealer for a personal test drive. And find out what's ahead for 1978...and beyond.

The new Futura.

FORD FAIRMONT FUTURA

SEE WHAT'S NEW TODAY IN A CHEVROLET.

Ford Fairmont Futura, 1978

Chevrolet, 1977

Behind the great name .

A car of classic elegance—with all the comfort, all the luxury, all the quality you expect of Cadillac. And yet, the 1978 Fleetwood Brougham (pictured), Coupe deVille and Sedan deVille are beautifully agile. Responsive. Lively. Maneuverable.

It's luxury all the way—but luxury you can feel good about. Because Cadillac 1978 is designed for efficient use of space, engineered for the changing world of today—while preserving traditional Cadillac legroom and headroom.

Cadillac, 1977

a great car.

The luxury leaders have arrived. See them. Drive them. And
or another kind of luxury, consider Seville by Cadillac . . . it
tands alone among the world's great cars. And the 1978
:ldorado with front-wheel drive and a flair all its own.

At your Cadillac dealer now.

Cadillac
1978

ECONOMY IS NOT OUR ONLY MISSION.

B-210 GX. 48 highway, 36 city. 1978 EPA estimates based on optional 5-speed manual transmission. Your mileage may differ, depending on how and where you drive, your car's condition and optional equipment. California/high-altitude mileage lower. But instead of miles per gallon, let us talk about years per car. Let us talk about another way Datsun saves — through quality. Every mile is comfortable, solid, enjoyable... because of these B-210 GX standards: steel-belted radials. Front disc brakes (power, of course). Fully reclining bucket seats. Full wheel covers. Plus optional 5-speed stick and racy stripes. All wrapped in an all-steel, all-welded unibody. It's Datsun, dedicated — driven — to deliver the greatest economy of all: quality.

NOBODY DEMANDS MORE FROM A DATSUN THAN DATSUN.

DATSUN.
WE ARE DRIVEN.

"Hang tough, Datsun!"

DATSUN'S NEW ECONOMY WAGON MAKES YOU FEEL RICH.

The amazing 210, Datsun's lowest-priced wagon.

Long. Graceful. Roomy. The new 210 Sportwagon doesn't scrimp to help you save. In fit...in finish...in ride...you sense that everything works and will keep working.

Allow yourself a private moment inside the 210's inspired interior. Stretch out, lean back, stroke and touch. Listen to the quiet. An all-steel unibody and extra insulation lock out rattles and road noise. (Finicky? Yes. But that's what "driven" means.)

Virtually all the comforts you could want in any car are <u>standard</u> in this economy wagon, yet often <u>extra</u> on some others: reclining front bucket seats, power front disc brakes, side window defoggers, rear window defroster, stalk-mounted controls and more. All built in by a company that's been crafting quality cars for nearly half a century: Nissan Motor Company, Ltd.

Buy or lease the new 210 today. It's rich, not expensive.

39 MPG HWY **28** MPG CITY

1979 EPA estimate for comparisons. Optional 5-speed. Your mileage may differ, depending on how and where you drive, condition of car and optional equipment.

Split rear seat folds down to accommodate passenger and long cargo.

NOBODY DEMANDS MORE

DATSUN
WE ARE DRIVEN

NISSAN

INTRODUCING THE NEW BREED

Presenting a whole New Breed of Mustang for '79. Dramatic new sports car styling gives this Mustang one of the most efficient aerodynamic designs of any car now built in America. Mustang's precise handling helps it flatten corners. Choose from four engines: a standard 2.3 litre overhead cam, and options of V-6, V-8 ..even a Turbocharged Mustang. And with all this, Mustang is still sticker priced to help you bring one home, in 2- or 3-door models. Capture one at your Ford Dealer now.

FORD MUSTANG

FORD DIVISION *Ford*

FORD MUSTANG '79

Ford Mustang, 1979

The new Toyota Celica. It's here now. A car which meets or exceeds all 1980 Federal fuel economy and safety standards. The latest in Toyota engineering advancements and wind tunnel refinements have produced an aerodynamic work of art. The Celica GT Liftback (pictured), GT and ST Sport Coupes.

A beautiful car and a fine machine. The GT Liftback aerodynamics have contributed to increased interior room (4" at shoulders), stability, acceleration and efficiency. The handling formula includes MacPherson strut front suspension, power assisted front disc brakes, and steel belted radials. The Celica's cockpit instrumentation is a beautiful example of functional engineering. And comfort is exemplified by the reclining bucket seats with newly designed adjustable driver's seat lumbar support.

The beauty is value. The 1978 Celica GT Liftback delivers Toyota dependability and economy. In EPA tests the Celica GT Liftback was rated at 34 highway, 20 city. These EPA ratings are estimates. Your mileage will vary depending on your driving habits and your car's condition and equipment. California ratings will be lower. GT Liftback options are for personal taste. Like power steering, automatic transmission or the new sun roof (available Jan. 1978). The 1978 Celica. The car of the 80's here today.

THE 1980's CELICA

YOU GOT IT.

TOYOTA

© Toyota Motor Sales, U.S.A., Inc. 1977

Toyota Celica, 1979

50s Cars
Ed. Jim Heimann / Flexi-cover,
192 pp. / € 6.99 / $ 9.99 /
£ 4.99 / ¥ 1500.00

60s Cars
Tony Thacker, Ed. Jim Heimann /
Flexi-cover, 192 pp. / € 6.99 /
$ 9.99 / £ 4.99 / ¥ 1500.00

Hot Rods & Custom Cars
Tony Thacker, Ed. Coco
Shinomiya / Flexi-cover,
192 pp. / € 6.99 / $ 9.99 /
£ 4.99 / ¥ 1500.00

"A collection of rare photos, advertisements, and other visual ephemera that's all about soupin'-up coupes." —*CityBeat*, Los Angeles

"Buy them all and add some pleasure to your life."

African Style
Ed. Angelika Taschen

Alchemy & Mysticism
Alexander Roob

All-American Ads 40s
Ed. Jim Heimann

All-American Ads 50s
Ed. Jim Heimann

All-American Ads 60s
Ed. Jim Heimann

American Indian
Dr. Sonja Schierle

Angels
Gilles Néret

Architecture Now!
Ed. Philip Jodidio

Art Now
Eds. Burkhard Riemschneider,
Uta Grosenick

Atget's Paris
Ed. Hans Christian Adam

Berlin Style
Ed. Angelika Taschen

Cars of the 50s
Ed. Jim Heimann, Tony
Thacker

Cars of the 60s
Ed. Jim Heimann, Tony
Thacker

Cars of the 70s
Ed. Jim Heimann, Tony
Thacker

Chairs
Charlotte & Peter Fiell

Christmas
Ed. Jim Heimann, Steven Heller

Classic Rock Covers
Ed. Michael Ochs

Design Handbook
Charlotte & Peter Fiell

Design of the 20th Century
Charlotte & Peter Fiell

Design for the 21st Century
Charlotte & Peter Fiell

Devils
Gilles Néret

Digital Beauties
Ed. Julius Wiedemann

Robert Doisneau
Ed. Jean-Claude Gautrand

East German Design
Ralf Ulrich / Photos: Ernst Hedler

Egypt Style
Ed. Angelika Taschen

Encyclopaedia Anatomica
Ed. Museo La Specola
Florence

M.C. Escher

Fashion
Ed. The Kyoto Costume
Institute

Fashion Now!
Ed. Terry Jones, Susie Rushton

Fruit
Ed. George Brookshaw,
Uta Pellgrü-Gagel

HR Giger
HR Giger

Grand Tour
Harry Seidler

Graphic Design
Eds. Charlotte & Peter Fiell

Greece Style
Ed. Angelika Taschen

Halloween
Ed. Jim Heimann, Steven
Heller

Havana Style
Ed. Angelika Taschen

Homo Art
Gilles Néret

Hot Rods
Ed. Coco Shinomiya, Tony
Thacker

Hula
Ed. Jim Heimann

Indian Style
Ed. Angelika Taschen

India Bazaar
Samantha Harrison, Bari Kumar

Industrial Design
Charlotte & Peter Fiell

Japanese Beauties
Ed. Alex Gross

Krazy Kids' Food
Eds. Steve Roden,
Dan Goodsell

Las Vegas
Ed. Jim Heimann,
W. R. Wilkerson III

London Style
Ed. Angelika Taschen

Mexicana
Ed. Jim Heimann

Mexico Style
Ed. Angelika Taschen

Morocco Style
Ed. Angelika Taschen

New York Style
Ed. Angelika Taschen

Paris Style
Ed. Angelika Taschen

Penguin
Frans Lanting

20th Century Photography
Museum Ludwig Cologne

Photo Icons I
Hans-Michael Koetzle

Photo Icons II
Hans-Michael Koetzle

Pierre et Gilles
Eric Troncy

Provence Style
Ed. Angelika Taschen

Robots & Spaceships
Ed. Teruhisa Kitahara

Safari Style
Ed. Angelika Taschen

Seaside Style
Ed. Angelika Taschen

Albertus Seba. Butterflies
Irmgard Müsch

**Albertus Seba. Shells &
Corals**
Irmgard Müsch

Signs
Ed. Julius Wiedeman

South African Style
Ed. Angelika Taschen

Starck
Philippe Starck

Surfing
Ed. Jim Heimann

Sweden Style
Ed. Angelika Taschen

Sydney Style
Ed. Angelika Taschen

Tattoos
Ed. Henk Schiffmacher

Tiffany
Jacob Baal-Teshuva

Tiki Style
Sven Kirsten

Tuscany Style
Ed. Angelika Taschen

Valentines
Ed. Jim Heimann,
Steven Heller

Web Design: Best Studios
Ed. Julius Wiedemann

Web Design: Flash Sites
Ed. Julius Wiedemann

Web Design: Portfolios
Ed. Julius Wiedemann

**Women Artists
in the 20th and 21st Century**
Ed. Uta Grosenick